mi·lieu

/mil'yo͞o,mil'yə(r)/

JARED U. BALMER, PhD
R. MICHAEL BULLOCH, LCSW
W. KIMBALL DELAMARE, LCSW

mi·lieu

/mil'yōō,mil'yə(r)/

THE MAKING *of a* THERAPEUTIC ENVIRONMENT

PROBLEM FORMATIONS *and* PROBLEM RESOLUTIONS

Published by Advantage, Charleston, South Carolina.
Member of Advantage Media Group.

ADVANTAGE is a registered trademark, and the Advantage colophon is a trademark of Advantage Media Group, Inc.

Printed in the United States of America.

10 9 8 7 6 5 4 3 2 1

ISBN: 978-1-64225-343-6
LCCN: 2021920859

Cover design by David Taylor.
Layout design by Wesley Strickland.

This publication is designed to provide accurate and authoritative information in regard to the subject matter covered. It is sold with the understanding that the publisher is not engaged in rendering legal, accounting, or other professional services. If legal advice or other expert assistance is required, the services of a competent professional person should be sought.

Advantage Media Group is proud to be a part of the Tree Neutral® program. Tree Neutral offsets the number of trees consumed in the production and printing of this book by taking proactive steps such as planting trees in direct proportion to the number of trees used to print books. To learn more about Tree Neutral, please visit **www.treeneutral.com**.

Advantage Media Group is a publisher of business, self-improvement, and professional development books and online learning. We help entrepreneurs, business leaders, and professionals share their Stories, Passion, and Knowledge to help others Learn & Grow. Do you have a manuscript or book idea that you would like us to consider for publishing? Please visit **advantagefamily.com**.

This book is dedicated to all who work in the milieu.

You spend countless hours encouraging, teaching, and believing in those who feel lost, discouraged, and defeated.

The difference you make—makes all the difference.

Contents

Introduction

The Problem

Mental health issues are ubiquitous. Virtually all adults can point to a person suffering from mental health issues within their immediate or extended family circles. No one can doubt that mental health problems have woven themselves into our social fabric with increasing strength.

The National Alliance of Mental Health (NAMH) estimates that around one in five adults in the United States—43.8 million, or 18.5 percent—experience mental illness in a given year. Approximately one in twenty-five adults in the United States—9.8 million, or 4.0 percent—experience a serious mental illness in a given year that substantially interferes with or limits one or more major life activities.

Additionally, the gathering storm clouds of mental illness among our young are particularly worrisome. Over the past decade, these clouds have grown ever darker, with public agencies and media reporting a sharp rise in suicide among teens. In September of 2020, the World Health Organization reported that one in six people between the ages of ten and nineteen experience mental health problems. Attempts at suicide and self-harm ideation are only part of the overall crisis. Mental health diagnoses—like neurodevelopmental, bipolar, depressive, anxiety, OCD, trauma, eating, and substance-related disorders, just to name a few—are all part and parcel of the mental health tsunami washing over our young.

Lifetime Prevalence of Any Mental Disorder Among Adolescents (2001-2004) *Data from the National Comorbidity Survey Adolescent Supplement (NCS-A)*

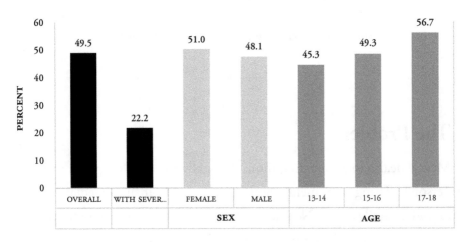

Treatment Options

Unfortunately, not all individuals affected with mental health issues receive regular treatment by qualified professionals. According to the National Alliance of Mental Health (NAMH), approximately 60 percent of adults and 50 percent of youth receive no treatment for their mental health problems. These statistics, decried by all those interested in the emotional well-being of persons who suffer from mental illness, are seated in a host of underlying variables. Frequently, cited reasons are fear and shame—the ever-present stigmas associated with seeking psychiatric help. Other reasons include distrust in the professionals, hopelessness, and lack of insight. Among youth with behavior and addictive problems, outright denial is often indicated for treatment refusal. In addition, practical barriers such as lack of third-party payment, reliable transportation, work schedules, etc., may also be contributing factors that make up the statistics of those who do not receive regular treatment.

For those who seek help with their mental health problems, a wide variety of treatment options exist. They range from bibliotherapy to professional help, from low to high intensity, from low to high frequency, from outpatient to inpatient care, and from psychopharmacological to homeopathic treatment. Among the large collection of treatment options, a sizable number of interventions are delivered in a group format. In fact, utilizing "the group" to assist in the support, shaping, and modification of individual behavior has proven to be effective across the globe.

- Throughout the United States—in fact, worldwide—people with common problems and challenges have created self-help groups. Overeaters Anonymous (OA), Children and Adults with Attention-Deficit/Hyperactivity Disorder (CHADD), and Depression and Bipolar Support Alliance (DBSA) are just a small sample of the pervasiveness of these organizations. The reason for the effectiveness of these groups lies in the fact that people with like challenges can significantly empathize, support, bring hope, add strategies, hold each other responsible, and help each other in the coping and healing processes.

- Group processes without leadership by a mental health professional are found across the social spectrum. Levels of motivation are improved around a Boy Scout campfire. Productivity changes as a result of an ad hoc work group in a factory. And learning processes grow more optimal following group meetings of the Parent–Teacher Association.

- Group therapy, conducted by mental health professionals, is a standard staple in a variety of settings, including group homes, wilderness therapy, therapeutic boarding schools, intensive outpatient treatment, residential treatment centers, psychiatric hospitals, etc. The power of the group has proven to be particularly effective among adolescents whose developmental stage renders them highly susceptible to peer influence.

The Power of Group Interaction

Behavior has no opposites. There is no such thing as nonbehavior. Therefore, one cannot *not* behave. This fact is the core reason for the shaping power of the individual within group interaction. Why? As soon as two or more people meet, they immediately begin to exchange cues in an attempt to define the nature of their relationship. These cues will *always* include nonverbal—and may include verbal—behavior. All behavior, nonverbal and verbal alike, exchanged between two or more individuals represents cues to influence each other's behavior. It follows that since one cannot *not* communicate, one cannot *not* influence others.

Example: Persons A and B are crossing each other on a city sidewalk. As they get closer to the crossing, each individual engages in nonverbal cues as to which side the crossing should occur—the left or right. Both individuals are attempting to influence each other. In a country where traffic is right sided, the "negotiation" for crossing each other may be easily resolved. However, such crossing attempts may be more complicated for individuals from countries where traffic patterns are opposite from what we might consider "normal."

In any group, formal or informal, small or large, group members exchange tens of thousands of nonverbal and verbal cues to define the natures of their relationships. To be precise, Person A, by his or her verbal and nonverbal exchange with Person B, may attempt to define that relationship differently than with Person C. Thus, each group member will eventually arrive at multiple dyadic relationships with all the individual group participants.

> Groups are powerful. The collective influence of group members on a single individual cannot be overstated. Groups, formal or informal, can have healing, empowering, motivational, and prosocial properties.

Groups are powerful. The collective influence of group members on a single individual cannot be overstated. Groups, formal or informal, can have healing, empowering, motivational, and prosocial properties. Conversely, they may have devastating effects by persuading members to drink the "toxic Kool-Aid." The same operational dynamics are applicable to any group of people, regardless of how they define themselves: casual, structured, formal, informal, loose, close knit, or overwise.

For example, families may sit down collectively for a discussion—a group meeting of sorts. Yet outside of the sleeping hours, family members interact continuously. (Remember, one cannot *not* communicate, and one cannot *not* influence others.) The collective interaction among them, the multiplicity of dyadic relationships, renders them with a host of spoken and unspoken, implicit, and explicit "rules of the road"—the making of the family environment.

Therefore, when a person inquires of another, "Tell me about your family," they seek information regarding the fabric of the family environment or the family milieu—the physical or social setting in which something occurs or develops.

The Making of a Therapeutic Environment

Leadership teams of any organization, which may include the city council, an NBA team, or any other endless collections of formal or informal groups, all have an environment or a milieu. It is impossible not to have a "group climate" or a milieu. Regardless of how long such individuals meet, for only ten minutes or over the course of ten years, the group environment is characterized by relationships being formed and reformed through the never-ending process of influencing each other.

The fact that the milieu of any group can significantly influence a single member has long been universally recognized and cuts across any culture. In particular, it demands increased attention from laypersons and professionals who are in charge of creating and maintaining a purposeful environment—a therapeutic milieu, if you will. In an informal group without direction and specific leadership, the milieu will spontaneously come to life. However, in a formal group, the facilitator is charged with influencing the milieu in a productive, therapeutic direction. Thus, classroom teachers, shift supervisors, coaches, and group therapists, including an endless list of group leaders, all attempt to orchestrate the collective interaction of all participants toward a goal: a prosocial, positive, growth-promoting goal—a therapeutic milieu.

It must be recognized that the milieu of a group of individuals is also determined by the interactions that exist outside the formal group. It is then possible that the same collection of individuals operates in two milieus: one in the formal group and another outside the formal guidelines and parameters set by the sanctioned leader. For example, in the clinician-led group, cursing at each other is "outlawed." Yet outside that milieu, individuals may pepper each other with insults and, hence, create a different milieu. This phenomenon takes on heightened significance in residential treatment settings where individuals operate in relatively close proximity and spend extensive time interacting. This truth—the existence of the potential for two different milieus—has long been recognized by those who operate mental health hospitals, intensive outpatient programs, residential treatment centers, therapeutic boarding schools, and outdoor behavioral health programs.

In all such settings, formal groups are conducted under the direct leadership of mental health clinicians, dorm counselors, houseparents, and other members of the staff. However, the totality of formal individual and group interaction is limited. In a residential setting, the one-on-one or group therapy interaction for a given client with the professional staff typically varies from one to eight hours per week. The rest of the waking hours are spent in interaction with the childcare and teaching staff. Collectively, the staff is implementing and maintaining a therapeutic milieu. The core values of such a community are always based on support, respect, caring, honesty, and accountability. Aside from the formal and casual interactions between client and staff are the interactions between the clients *without* the direct supervision of the staff. This may have the potential for creating a different milieu—one that may be counterproductive or even toxic.

Crafting and maintaining such an environment is no easy task. It requires skill. Exceptional skills are particularly required when working with a population that is resistant to change. Adolescent and young adult populations that are prodded and coaxed into treatment by parents or the court system often display a fair amount of resistance. Such resistance is often based on projection—finding blame for maladaptive behavior outside of themselves. Regardless of the population served, establishing and maintaining a therapeutic milieu requires know-how.

The Purpose of This Book

The effectiveness of any purposeful group is inevitably based on the health status of its milieu. If the milieu of a group population is toxic, the overall objectives are compromised. Conversely, a healthy milieu is often the key variable that accounts for a positive outcome. The purpose of this book is to identify and consider seven essential elements that are seminal in the formation and maintenance of a healthy milieu. These elements find particular application to child, adolescent, and young adult groups. However, the same elements find application for any milieu, formal, therapeutic, informal, or casual.

> The effectiveness of any purposeful group is inevitably based on the health status of its milieu.

- **Chapter 1: Know Your Audience!**
  Matching the Age, Maturity, and Motivational Levels of Group Members with the Rules and Guidelines of the Client Community

- **Chapter 2: Integrity and Accountability**
  Assuring That Vision and Policy Are Aligned with Day-to-Day Operations

- **Chapter 3: Cooking on All Burners**
  Maintaining an Optimal Measuring System of Progress across the Different Stages of Change

- **Chapter 4: Weather Forecasting**
  Anticipating Situations in Which the Culture Is Most Vulnerable for Negative Influence and Deterioration

- **Chapter 5: Starve the Rogue**
  Dealing with the Negative "Power Broker"

- **Chapter 6: Managing the Underground**
  Learning Lessons from Distractive Forces

- **Chapter 7: Keeping the Bogeyman Away**
  Maintaining a Thriving Milieu through Optimal Staff-Management Practices

It is not necessary to read these chapters in consecutive order. They are freestanding and can be read in any order one wishes.

CHAPTER 1

Know Your Audience!

Matching the Age, Maturity, and Motivational Levels of Group
Members with the Rules and Guidelines of the Client Community

JARED U. BALMER

C REATING AN ENVIRONMENT THAT IS BASED ON SUPPORT, predictability, dignity, and respect for the clients is the genesis of all therapeutic endeavors. It is the foundation, but that alone is not enough. A milieu that undertakes the task of changing behavior must consider the variability of the presenting problems: the age, maturity, clinical presentation, and motivational levels of the client population. A group of young adults is a very different "animal" than a group of latency age children. While a group of drug-dependent adolescents may show significant levels of treatment-interfering behavior, a therapeutic population troubled by depression would face a different set of challenges.

> Knowing your audience is seminal to creating and maintaining an environment of change.

11

Therefore, knowing your audience is seminal to creating and maintaining an environment of change.

The Problem: The Right Reward?

The leadership of a transitional living center serving a coed young adult population was confronted with a problem. After operating for over a year, the clinical staff noticed that the client handbook was heavily weighted in addressing maladaptive behavior with corresponding consequences. Delineations of rewards for prosocial behavior were sparse. The leadership team concluded that this trend toward a more negative approach was a major contributing factor for the relatively small group of clients on the highest level of the milieu-level system. This resulted in the unanimous decision to add incentives or rewards for "good" behavior. As a result, a closet in the cafeteria was converted into a candy bar store. In tandem, a newly developed client handbook described how a client can be rewarded with a candy bar. The criteria were based on demonstrating specific prosocial behaviors that benefited the individual and/or the client community. After several months, the center's leadership noticed only a small change in the number of clients on the upper-milieu-level system—prompting yet another problem-solving meeting. They found that the majority of client consumers of the candy bars were largely restricted to a few eighteen-year-olds; not many of the older clients responded to the candy incentive. The ensuing problem-solving discussion concluded that cashing in on a candy bar was too difficult, and consequently, the requirements for the candy reward were lowered. After two months, the staff noticed that the candy consumption relatively stayed the same—resulting in no appreciable change in distribution to clients along the milieu-level system. A puzzled staff was looking for answers.

CONSIDERATIONS FOR SOLUTIONS

Behavior theorists, researchers, and clinicians have written volumes on shaping behavior. The work of B. F. Skinner (1953) makes it clear that one of the most effective methods for strengthening a behavior is through positive reinforcement—the presentation of anything that the individual views as a reward. All reinforcers (the things that the individual views as rewarding) fall into one of two categories. Primary reinforcers involve biological importance such as food, water, sleep, air, sex, etc. Secondary reinforcers are all things the individual views as rewarding *beyond* biological needs. These reinforcers may be money, vacation, forms of entertainment, etc. Social reinforcers, a subcategory of secondary reinforcers, are particularly powerful in shaping human behavior. They may include such things as smiles, acceptance, praise, acclaim, attention from other people, reward letters, and so forth. For some individuals, simply being in the presence of others can be a social reinforcer.

Primary reinforcers such as food hold greater attraction to children than to older adolescents, young adults, and adults. Intermittent praise from the boss for doing a great job is significantly more valuable in shaping behavior than receiving a turkey for Christmas. Conversely, offering the child a sucker may very well be greater motivation to wash the dishes than "Mommy would be so happy if you would wash the dishes." Of course, this does not mean that more mature individuals do not respond to primary reinforcers. However, older adolescents and adults respond better to behavior change when socially reinforced. In clearly stated terms, the issues in the above-described case would likely be improved by implementing social reinforcers rather than candy bars. Find reinforcers that adapt and work for the group.

The Problem: The Right Motivation

A coeducational adolescent residential treatment center specializing in substance-abuse recovery has been operating for only a short time. Virtually all clients referred to the center by their respective parents exhibited much resistance to entering the program. Adolescents typically do not voluntarily submit to treatment for chemical or alcohol abuse. Many client profiles describe significant parent–child conflict. When staff quizzed newly admitted clients regarding the reason for admission, the answers usually involved laying blame on others. In fact, these clients were almost universally projecting their difficulties outside themselves. If it was not the parents' fault, then it was some other authority figure. Therefore, problem ownership was not a readily observable phenomenon. Because of this fact, program leadership was anxious to create a therapeutic milieu that would foster personal accountability. This was a critically significant building block in the rehabilitation effort.

A voluminous client manual was produced. It contained a lengthy list of maladaptive behaviors, ranging from dishonesty to outright oppositionality. Juxtaposed among these infractions and treatment-interfering behaviors was an equally long list of rewards for *not* engaging in these self-defeating behaviors. It was reasoned that the rewards for not engaging in maladaptive behavior would provide the motivation to abandon it.

Some eight months into operation, the clinical team reported the following findings:

- Approximately 50 percent of the adolescent population showed significant improvements in the reduction of treatment-interfering behaviors. For those clients, it appeared the milieu program hit a home run. Treatment-interfering behavior decreased, and compliance with prosocial behavior increased.

- For the rest of the population, the result was unfavorable. There was no appreciable reduction in maladaptive behavior.

Puzzled with these results, the clinical team engaged in an extended discussion on how to increase the percentage of clients responding to programmatic rewards. They decided to expand the rewards, such as free time, off-campus activities, the ability to order in personal favorite foods, movie nights, etc. Some six months later, however, there was still no significant change in the results.

CONSIDERATIONS FOR SOLUTIONS

Researchers and clinicians like Erikson, Kohlberg, and Piaget have provided extensive insight into the cognitive, emotional, motivational, and moral development of children, adolescents, and adults. Explaining causality for motivation for such age groups is contingent on a host of developmental variables. Historically, studies on motivation have primarily focused on why adolescents engage in maladaptive behaviors. It is only in the last two decades that an increasing number of clinicians and researchers are dealing with understanding the motivation of why adolescents *avoid* maladaptive behavior (Hardy et al. 2015). The variables influencing the motivation for avoiding negative behavior changes evolve during childhood and adolescence

> When it comes to identifying motivational factors for teenagers that reinforce both prosocial and maladaptive behavior, peer feedback and influence cannot be overstated.

and are based on psychosocial development. For example, a morally mature adolescent may avoid certain behaviors because he or she classifies such behavior as morally wrong or against the law. A child with underdeveloped maturity may not view the same behavior through the glasses of moral or legal consequences. More likely, avoiding parental punishment trumps a highly developed moral code, as does a reward for not "being bad."

When it comes to identifying motivational factors for teenagers that reinforce both prosocial and maladaptive behavior, peer feedback and influence cannot be overstated. The professional literature is ablaze with this fact. Moreover, parents and teachers can speak with authority concerning this phenomenon. At no other time does peer influence have a bigger footprint on identity formation than during the teen years. Such peer influence comes through praise, acknowledgment, and the heightened need for acceptance and belonging—in short, the *adolescent wants to be liked.*

The figure on the next page shows the percentages of reward factors linked to maladaptive behaviors in childhood latency versus the adolescent-aged youth. It shows that most adolescents avoid maladaptive behavior for one of three reasons: to gain a reward, to be liked, or to avoid moral or legal issues. Most heavily weighted is the need to be liked.

LATENCY AGE			ADOLESCENT AGE		
Stage 1	Avoiding maladaptive behavior to avoid *punishment*	25%	Stage 2	Avoiding maladaptive behavior to gain a *reward* attached for "not doing it"	20%
Stage 2	Avoiding maladaptive behavior to gain a *reward* for "not doing it"	65%	Stage 3	Avoiding maladaptive behavior because "I want people to *like* me"	65%
			Stage 4	Avoiding maladaptive behavior because it is morally wrong or against the *law*	12%

Reasons that 50 percent of the client population did not respond to the rewards offered for avoiding maladaptive behavior are likely to be found in the issues discussed above. In all probability, the client population was composed of younger adolescents (Latency Age Stage 2 and Adolescent Age Stage 2) and older clients (primarily in Adolescent Age Stage 3). The older population reacts to discarding inappropriate behavior not to gain rewards but to meet the overwhelming need to be liked by their peers.

In the attempt to decrease treatment-interfering behavior, creating an environment where adolescents experience *being liked by their peers* may have been more fruitful. This becomes operational when the teenager abandons maladaptive behavior because giving up such behavior garners more kudos from the peer group—in short, "*I'll change my behavior because I want to be liked.*" Understandably, this is only possible if the climate among the peers defines prosocial behavior as "cool" and maladaptive behavior as "lame." Anyone who operates a therapeutic milieu knows this is not an easy task. Bringing about such a climate is challenging for the staff, made more difficult with a rolling admission of new arrivals who, with negative attitudes, are resolutely committed to "sex, drugs, and rock and roll." The affirmative influences and reinforcers of the milieu producing the mantra that "positive is cool" must be stronger than the potential negative force of the "underground."

Do not fear—help is on the way. A more in-depth discussion about this issue is found in chapter 6 ("Managing the Underground").

The Problem: The Right Ingredient?

A residential treatment center opened its doors for business. The targeted client population was adolescent boys with behavior problems, such as oppositional defiant disorder, low self-esteem, dysthymia, and child–parent discord. Many of the boys had histories of chemical abuse. The overwhelming majority of the clients came from large urban centers like New York City, Miami, Los Angeles, etc. The program was located on what was originally a two-hundred-acre horse farm. Intending to make good use of the open, farmlike surroundings, the center's leadership wasted no time developing an equestrian component. Each boy was provided with his personal horse and received professional instructions on becoming a horse whisperer. In addition, all clients participated in regional roping competitions. Short of conducting a cattle drive, the boys were groomed to be cowboys. Even with the less pleasant tasks, such as shoveling manure, this was the Rolls-Royce of equestrian programs. Any visitors to the program were introduced to the boys, who in turn were jumping at the bit to demonstrate their horse-handling skills. It was obvious these clients were very proud of their achievements. While the clients participated in individual, group, and family therapy, the time involvement of the equestrian component essentially defined the therapeutic milieu. After two years of operation, the program's leadership was puzzled by the fact they were unable to attract enough students to fill the twenty-four beds. Reviewing all the operational statistics, it was noted that the conversion rate—the comparison of program visits by parents of prospective students compared to the actual number of admissions—was extremely low. Dedicating more resources to the marketing programs did not improve the conversion rate. Puzzlement turned into frustration. The program had competent clinicians, an attractive setting, a respectable education program, and a state-of-the-art equestrian program. What gives?

CONSIDERATIONS FOR SOLUTIONS

When admitting an adolescent to a residential treatment program, the parent is also "enrolled." In some cases, a referring professional who recommended the placement to the parent is also a stakeholder in the treatment process. Therefore, for every enrollment, at a minimum, two consumers are admitted and possibly a third one—the referring professional. In virtually all cases, parents of children of all ages will personally visit the treatment program before a placement decision is made. They scope out the setting, getting a feel for the environment and the staff, assessing whether the program can effectively address the needs of their child, and in all cases, imagine the end from the beginning. Much thought is given to the following questions: Will my child make the desired changes, and how will the newly acquired skills be transferred to the home environment? With this in mind, a parent living in Manhattan or San Francisco cannot imagine how cowboy skills can benefit their child. Regardless of the child's enthusiasm for bonding with a horse or mastering team-roping skills, a parent may justifiably struggle to understand how these skills will profit the child in the future. While the parent may see the benefit of the child learning how to work and putting effort into something that aids in recovery, the likelihood of the child continuing in the gentle art of horse husbandry is practically zero. The habituation of such positive traits as working hard, following through, or finding success in the face of obstacles can be acquired in other settings. In short, some parents may have difficulty visualizing how all these cowboy skills can find application in a large metropolitan area of the country.

There are many successful therapeutic programs with an ancillary component. In creating a therapeutic milieu with supplemental programing, one must not lose sight of the parents' psychosocial makeup. They are as much a consumer as the client. In most cases, the parents choose the program and not the child. Rather than the abovementioned program, an outdoor adventure program that includes a host of recreational activities may be more suitable. Why? Because it has transferable value. The child, with the possible inclusion of parents and other family members, can easily continue in these activities following discharge. There is nothing wrong with horse and rope training. Worthy benefits can be seen in this type of therapy, but accomplishments like rock climbing, mountain biking, trekking, skiing, etc., may simply have longer legs.

> Ancillary services should not overshadow the core clinical services. Promoting the core must remain the major feature of the program.

In creating a comprehensive therapeutic program, one must not fall prey to the "tail wagging the dog" phenomenon. Ancillary services should not overshadow the core clinical services. Promoting the core must remain the major feature of the program. Parents who are lured into placement decisions by designer services may find themselves disappointed with the final outcomes and often place blame on the service provider.

The Problem: Individual Differences versus Group Integrity

At a monthly staff meeting, the supervisor of a childcare staff voices a number of concerns. She indicates that more and more clients are raising questions about the "rules of the road" for the milieu. In some cases, outright anger and defiance bubble to the surface. Many of the complaints center on fairness—voices like, "Why do I have to do it, and my roommate doesn't?" or "Why does everybody have to jump through the same hoops, even though we are dealing with very different issues?" In response to these concerned questions, the leadership of the facility calls on specific members from different departments to conduct an analysis of the root cause of the disturbance in the milieu. A clinician, teacher, recreational therapist, and staff member were faced with the following facts:

- The age distribution of clients was fourteen through nineteen years of age.

- Presenting problems of the client population included depression, dysthymia, anxiety, drug abuse, some sexual acting out, low self-esteem, reactive attachment disorder, ADHD, and a few cases of obsessive-compulsive disorder.

- The average length of stay ranged from six months to eighteen months.

- The milieu program guidelines consisted of a small book of forty-eight pages. It contained rules and guidelines regarding grooming and hygiene standards, search policies, core and ancillary rules of acceptable and nonacceptable behaviors, consequences for rule violations, table manners, standards for keeping personal spaces orderly, lists of community chores in which all must participate, seating arrangements when transporting a group of clients in the facility vehicles, and rules for when a client is eligible for a home visit—just to name a few.

As part of the findings of the root-cause analysis, the leadership team discovered rules and guidelines were not specific to the presenting problem of individuals among the client groups. In other words, the ubiquitous questions of unfairness among the client population were not addressed in the milieu handbook. The fourteen-year-old boy suffering from depression with no history of chemical abuse does not, in reality, require a body search when returning from a home visit. To inspect the cleanliness and hygiene of the seventeen-year-old female suffering from contamination-based OCD may also be unnecessary. Yet her roommate may complain to the staff, "You always check my clothing drawers but never hers—this is not fair." The realities of impartiality encouraged a campaign of complaining among part of the client population that became infectious, giving rise to a number of maladaptive behaviors and threatening an overall breakdown in the therapeutic milieu.

CONSIDERATIONS FOR SOLUTIONS

A residential treatment program casting a wide net for admission criteria is saddled with creating a universal road map of acceptable and nonacceptable behaviors. This is often a task akin to a high-wire act. Programs such as this, addressing a wide variety of presenting problems and diagnostic categories and charged with implementing a therapeutic environment, must find a middle ground in addressing the needs of all clients. However, such a universal road map may not fit all clients equally well. Such challenges can be addressed in three ways.

- The core milieu rules must contain descriptions of prosocial and maladaptive behaviors to fit all clients, regardless of mental and behavioral health histories. Inappropriate sexual contact with others, aggression toward self and others, as well as further unsuitable behaviors, are listed as unacceptable, while prosocial behaviors, including good hygiene and cleaning up after oneself and others, come to mind. These generalized rules, which apply to all, are the beginnings of creating the "rules of the road." So where is the middle ground?

- Guarding against the breakdown of the milieu and arriving at the middle ground must include the programmatic consequences for the most maladaptive behaviors. Those consequences are there for everyone, but not everyone will come under their scrutiny. While compliance with daily tasks and social mores becomes the measuring device for progress, it must be noted that in the further development of the rules of the road, individuals with protracted histories of oppositional behaviors are required to live by more expanded rules than individuals suffering from complex clinical issues, anxiety, or mood disorders, but who are generally compliant. Both actually are required to live by the same rules, but those clients with overt acting-out behavior (e.g., lying, stealing, using contraband, being aggressive, having self-harm ideation, acting out sexually, etc.) demand the lion's share of staff time. Thus, the road map of the milieu for such clients and the staff who is charged to assist them benefits from clarity and detail. Paramount to this is client understanding that everyone enjoys the positive consequences of respect for rules, and consequently, anyone who engages in destructive or noncompliant behaviors deals with the consequences. Since the compliant client is not as impacted by the consequences of acting-out behaviors delineated in the client handbook, the middle ground is achieved.

- Because clients with acting-out behaviors demand much of the staff's time and support, the milieu has a tendency to be compliant driven. With such clients, progress, to a large extent, is measured by the relative compliant behavior. Yet individuals with acting-*in* problems (e.g., anxiety, OCD, mood disorder, dysthymia, etc.) benefit little from a therapeutic milieu that focuses on compliance. Consequently, the larger the diversification of diagnoses existing in any milieu, the more you will see a breakdown of overall therapeutic success. More time will be devoted to noncompliant and acting-out behaviors of clients who demand grease for the squeaky wheel. Such inordinate attention comes at the expense of those individuals who are cooperative and compliant. Thus, grouping client populations by presenting problems and diagnosis makes for a more meaningful milieu for individual clients.

The Problem: Knowing the End from the Beginning

The Sunshine Boarding School has been in operation for several years. The school is specializing in helping youth with some emotional baggage find success in life. The admission criteria exclude sex offenders, youth with histories of cruelty to animals, highly combative and aggressive students, and actively suicidal and intellectually disabled youth. The facility operates on a traditional school schedule defined by quarters and semesters. New incoming students are admitted and graduate only on certain dates, typically at the end of the fall and spring semesters. The minimum length of stay for each student is six semesters. Those who have completed this requirement typically graduate from the school in groups.

The milieu program has four levels. All admissions who matriculate at the same time move through the level program as a group. The progression from one level to the next takes place on a predetermined date so that the total length of stay is equally divided into four quadrants. In that regard, the school is similar to a traditional high school, where individual students are part of a graduation class, moving from freshman to senior classes as a group.

The administrators of the school have noticed a slow yet steady decline in the average daily census. An analysis of such a decline revealed three possible reasons. First, follow-up studies indicated that an appreciable number of program graduates "did not do well," according to parent feedback. Second, intermittent small groups of clients had been expelled from the school on account of multiple or significant infractions of program rules. Third, referrals to the school had declined.

CONSIDERATIONS FOR SOLUTIONS

Moving all clients through a program like a traditional high school places the main focus on the group, often at the expense of considering individual differences. Not all clients work through the progressive stages of change in unison. Age, maturity, history, and motivational levels beg for individual attention. Certain behavioral standards are rightfully demanded for level progression; however, not all clients reach that threshold simultaneously. This fact is further compromised by clients who demonstrate high levels of resistance to change. It is no surprise that such individuals have ways to connect with each other in creating a destructive "underground." These negatively charged individuals who are not ready for the next level of change have a devastating effect on the overall milieu. The dismissal of such a group of clients is symptomatic of a dysfunctional milieu. Repetitions of such group expulsions can signal the death sentence of a school unless major revisions are made, ranging from admission criteria to the very reworking of the milieu program. In general terms, the more diverse the client population, the more the milieu must focus on individual differences and the corresponding milieu rules and guidelines. Conversely, a homogeneous client population calls for less diversification in milieu rules. In both cases, maintaining a healthy milieu demands constant vigilance by the staff. Since not all clients rush to embrace prosocial behavior, such a task can be demanding.

Summary

The milieu rules and guidelines of any group must be tailored to the makeup of the participating individuals. Age, maturity level, cognitive abilities, motivation, histories of presenting problems, future initiatives, etc., must be adequately addressed in the formulation of a corrective environment. The problems tackled in this chapter touch the surface of issues related to the work of client change and productivity. No one said that maintaining a successful therapeutic business is easy. Each requires vigilance and constant reconsiderations. Aiming and achieving a stable, predictable milieu is the foundation but often is not sufficient to address the diverse manifestation of problem behaviors. Hence, an effective milieu program aims to cater to the unique behavioral manifestations of a given diagnostic category and age group. In that regard, a client with a severe social phobia who avoids attending a group session must have different milieu implications and consequences than a client with an eating disorder. Yet the consequences for stealing from peers are equally applicable to both clients. Therefore, having a fundamental understanding of one's audience is the foundation of creating and maintaining a successful therapeutic setting.

References

Balmer, J. U., and R. M. Bulloch. "The Perfect Storm; Anxiety and Depression in Adolescents in the 21st Century." *Journal of Therapeutic Schools & Programs* VI, no. I (2013), https://natsap.org/pdfs/jtsp/vol6/6_article_3.pdf.

Hardy, S. A., D. C. Dollahite, N. Johnson, and J. B. Christensen. "Adolescent Motivations to Engage in Pro-Social Behaviors and Abstain from Health-Risk Behavior: A Self-Determination Theory Approach." *Journal of Personality* 83, no. 5 (October 2015), https://doi.org/10.1111/jopy.12123.

Skinner, B. F. *Science and Human Behavior*. New York: The Free Press, 1952.

CHAPTER 2

Integrity and Accountability

Assuring That Vision and Policy Are Aligned with Day-to-Day Operations

JARED U. BALMER

I T IS NOT A GIVEN THAT INTEGRITY AND ACCOUNTABILITY ARE spontaneous occurrences in any organization. You could argue that in the cutthroat business world, we see less and less of these principled traits. Every hour of the day, a multitude of factors is at work that may challenge the reliability and steady state of our own efforts. In the increasingly competitive business of helping human beings recover from debilitating issues, it is ever more important that organizations achieve optimal, responsible functioning. The integrity and accountability, or the lack thereof, within one service area of an organization can have a positive or detrimental effect on all parts of the business, including the milieu. As the milieu is the energy that drives the therapy, in this chapter we examine inside and outside sources that can negatively impact the stability and integrity of the milieu—and subsequently, the whole organization running it.

The Problem: Did the Program Staff Get the Memo?

Harry, an educational consultant, had a thriving practice in Houston, Texas. He specialized in placing adolescent youth with behavioral and mental health challenges in therapeutic boarding schools and residential treatment centers. In order to assist parents in the optimal selection of such a program, Harry made it his mission to turn over every rock as he evaluated a program. Such a process started with a review of the web page and ended with a two-to-four-hour on-site visit. In most cases, examining the web page provided only basic information. Outside the description of the population served, a common thread was the assurance that the staff cared a great deal about the individuals they served and provided a stable and predictable milieu. Colleagues provided further insights. However, the most revealing and accurate information was gained by the on-site visit—seeing is believing. By reviewing the Acme Program's website, Harry made a mental list of some of the key features the program offered. What stood out was the emphasis on a highly structured peer environment, the components of equestrian therapy and adventure education, and the opportunities for competitive team-sports involvement.

Harry's tour of the Acme School started with meeting the admissions director. She described the program in the same general terms communicated on the website. Two young men between the ages of fourteen and sixteen then escorted the visitor on a tour throughout the campus. Unfortunately, Harry came away with a different impression than what the website advertised. For a student population of eighty, two horses in the corral on the back property did not seem sufficient to suggest an equestrian component of the school. Moreover, only one tour guide indicated he had ridden a horse, but that was some two months ago. Equally disturbing for Harry was the discovery that the students, while having access to a basketball court, did not play in a competitive league, as was implied on the website. Yes, there was a lot of basketball played—but not competitively. Harry left the facility with a bad taste in his mouth and lots of questions for the administration about squaring the paper version with the real thing.

CONSIDERATIONS FOR SOLUTIONS

Many programs, as a value-added feature, offer adjunct programming. This may include such things as spiritual discovery, equestrian programming, volunteer work and community involvement, specific sport and recreation activities, technology and vocational programming, or exotic excursions abroad. Most of these activities are advertised to heighten the attractiveness of the program. And if the integrity of the activities holds up, they can certainly have therapeutic value. In some cases, however, such offerings mitigate parental guilt for sending their son or daughter away from home to a "happy place" in an otherwise seemingly rugged situation. In the end, these adjunct features may have vigorous implementation, but if they are not central to the core ideals and therapeutic methods, they are nothing more than creative embellishments. In deference to some, they can effectively provide a platform for various components of the core to unfold. However, it should be strongly reiterated that they are not the core. The core may include such things as the goals and objectives of the program, theoretical foundation of the treatment, and delineation of essential therapeutic services upon which the change process

> Again, everything flows, emanates, and arises from the core. The core represents that which defines a program.

31

is pivoting. All other policies and procedures flow from this core. Such aspects as the staffing pattern, the admission procedure, the behavioral-management techniques, and many others have to "wash" with the core. Again, everything flows, emanates, and arises from the core. The core represents that which defines a program. The core of a program must meet the child's fundamental clinical needs. Whether a program adds ballet or an equestrian or particular sports component, it should not be the decisive factor in the placement decision. While value-added programming has the potential to be a significant addition to core programing, when added for window dressing only, such additions can be detrimental to the overall effectiveness and integrity of the change institution.

The Problem: Institutional Drift

A residential treatment center with a coed adolescent population has been operating successfully for a number of years. A great deal of attention was given to developing programmatic rules and guidelines, both for the client population and for the childcare staff. Client meals were provided in a cafeteria. As expected, behavioral rules and guide-lines dictated client conduct in the dining room. Good table decorum was rewarded. Conversely, unacceptable behavior was associated with consequences. Throwing food, for instance, was a precursor to meals being served in the client's bedroom rather than the cafeteria. In such a case, three days of eating in the client's bedroom were indicated. The childcare staff would bring a meal tray to the client's bedroom.

Larry, a sixteen-year-old, had multiple food-throwing incidents in the cafeteria. After the third of these outbursts, it was obvious Larry had failed to learn from previous consequences. A staff member concluded that additional consequences were in order, so a tray with the lunch meal was delivered to Larry's bedroom. This time, however, one item was missing—a carton of milk.

A few months later, the clinical director looked in on a female client eating lunch in her bedroom. She noticed there was no milk carton anywhere. An inquiry among the childcare staff revealed that it had become a standard practice not to provide milk, but only water, to clients who eat their meals in their respective bedrooms.

CONSIDERATIONS FOR SOLUTIONS

In most cases, childcare staff members are not keeping manuals of programmatic rules and guidelines in their back pockets. Consequently, it may not be unusual for a caretaker to take matters into his or her own hands and overlook a small detail such as a carton of milk. After an initial familiarization of the rule book, new staff members often learn the ropes from observing staff with longer tenures. In this case, what was initiated by one employee became the standard. Some employees, motivated by good intentions, may add or change standard operating procedures. Some of these new and spontaneous standard changes may seem inconsequential. In the case of the missing milk, such an institutional drift could have more serious consequences. In most jurisdictions, withholding food as a consequence of maladaptive behavior is against the law.

A milieu is a living thing—never static. Forces to change the status quo are forever at work. Any facility is well served by monitoring the administration and consistent implementation of program guidelines in a hypervigilant fashion. Such an effort assures program integrity and avoids institutional drift.

The Problem: Renegade Maverick

The milieu of a therapeutic boarding school showed signs of stress. Frontline staff were taxed by daily applications of programmatic consequences for maladaptive behavior. A handful of students were repetitively at the receiving end of these sanctions. It appeared these kids had little concern for the outcome of rule breaking. This phenomenon was not unique to a particular class; it kept repeating itself with subsequent graduating classes.

The school leadership spent considerable time examining and reexamining milieu rules and guidelines. Adjustments were made not only throughout the academic year but also from year to year—with little or no change. The majority of students responded well to the guidelines. Yet an appreciable number chronically challenged many of the expectations set forth in the student handbook. In a desperate attempt to find a solution to this problem, the school leadership looked beyond the rule book. Admission criteria were examined in relation to the troublemakers; the conclusion was that they all fell within the accepted limits of admission parameters. The problem wasn't student pathology; it was something else.

Eventually, attention to finding a solution shifted to staff. During an in-depth interview with some of the errant students, the clinical director discovered valuable information. A comparative analysis of the feedback from all the interviews revealed the picture of an anti-establishment science teacher. Students were privileged to listen to a variety of comments aimed at questioning authority figures in general and school administrators in particular. A subsequent interview with the science teacher revealed that he did not agree with some of the rules and consequences for maladaptive student behavior. He was schooling a subgroup of clients in the art of oppositional defiance.

CONSIDERATIONS FOR SOLUTIONS

The need for congruency among the staff administering a program aimed at change cannot be overstated. In a therapeutic boarding school, where defiant recruits are easily taken in by countercultural ideals, all staff must understand and agree to the standards that make up the integrity of the program. Everyone is entitled to an opinion outside of the program, but inside the program, a lone power wolf can be a disastrous destabilizer to the milieu community. Another salient point to consider is the very students who find their ways through destabilizing cracks in the milieu can also be viewed as the hounds who can help root out the source of the cracks and discover those that need closure. Closing such holes cannot be accomplished by an administrative edict. As mentioned earlier, it requires full buy-in and subsequent enforcement by all employees and staff. This includes science teachers and *all* teachers, houseparents, frontline staff—even cooks and janitors. Accomplishing such a goal is typically achieved by three factors: (1) detailed, written standard operating procedures, (2) training sessions by those who developed the guidelines, and (3) modeling in real time. Implementation of those procedures will go a long way to facilitating a truly accountable milieu team.

The Problem: Keeper of the Flame

An emotional growth school enjoyed great success and popularity. The client population, consisting of adolescent boys and girls, showed significant improvement at discharge. Much of their success was attributed to the emotional growth curriculum developed by a founder of the school. It was her brainchild. To assure consistent implementation, the founder devoted much time to employee training. Such training primarily came in the form of lectures and modeling. Lecturing was enhanced through frequent use of a whiteboard, and modeling was done through real-time demonstrations of how to interact and intervene with clients. Intending to keep the institution pure, the founder was centrally involved in ongoing modeling and clarifying questions from the rank and file of employees. She was the "flame keeper." Any changes or modifications to the emotional growth curriculum required prior approval before implementation—for a good reason. The vision of the school was hers. Drifting away from that vision and the program implementation that flowed from it was crucial to the ongoing success of the school.

Unable to be everywhere, the founder selected a small handful of trusted employees who would share in those responsibilities. The daily implementation of the founder's vision was carefully implanted in the minds and actions of those few employees. Along with the founder, they became the keepers of the flame. They functioned as the inner circle of the operation—an honored position with a great deal of power.

An overseas assignment of the founder's spouse took her to a different country. Consequently, the school's board of directors replaced the founder with a new executive director. The new leader did not come up through the ranks of the school. He had leadership experiences in a variety of therapeutic schools and mental health settings but knew little about the inner workings of his new assignment. It was crucial that he learn the aims, objectives, and methodologies effecting change in the student population. He was anxious to read policies and procedures manuals. What he found was limited to a dress code and a daily schedule. Numerous meetings with the group of flame keepers contributed little to his understanding of the methods used to effect growth in the students. The magic piton for scaling the cliffs of change appeared to be locked away in the brains of the flame keepers. Whether through smug egotism, ambivalence, or pure laziness, it was obvious the flame keepers kept the precious bits and pieces of program functioning to themselves. This was a very fine and respected institution, but the combination of communication conflicts between the administration and youth mentors, along with a number of flame keepers finding other employment, eventually led to the demise of the school.

CONSIDERATIONS FOR SOLUTIONS

It is not uncommon for inventors and founders of all sorts to keep their know-how close to their chests. Their motivation to do so has many origins. Fear of competition, personal aggrandizement and adoration from others, and power may be at play. After all, who does not enjoy the accolades of being a guru? In deference to this mindset, many in this business have seen their hard work and ideas taken by trusted employees who leave to start their own programs. It happens. On the other hand, there are bright minds who displace fear or self-serving needs for good faith. They transmit their knowledge to the next generation in hopes of achieving permanency. However, if the new generation perceives that they are being coronated as flame keepers, viewing it as a great honor that calls for jealous protectionism, the genesis of a disaster is born. Keep in mind the definition of *flame keeper* as one who tends a fire that must be kept burning for the benefit of others or, in the expressed problem in this chapter segment, "one who keeps some idea alive."

> Setting standards by verbal instruction or modeling alone proves insufficient to standardize operations. Written policy and procedures manuals are required.

Committed to integrity and accountability, leaders of a complex operation with multiple employees and departments do best by setting standards. They cannot be murky, ill-defined procedures. Setting standards by verbal instruction or modeling alone proves insufficient to standardize operations. Written policy and procedures manuals are required. Such manuals ensure that all employees are familiar with the "secrets" of the know-how. This is particularly the case in departments that have the highest turnover within an organization. The foundation of solidifying consistency, integrity, and accountability throughout an organization is a well-defined, understandable, concise, and active living policy and procedures manual. Get the point? This manual should not only address the overall goal and objectives of the operation but also address the nitty-gritty of the interventions of the change process. All employees must be coronated to be keepers of the flame.

The Problem: Flexibility

The Sunshine Academy enjoyed a great deal of success. Its location, a stone's throw away from the Pacific Ocean, gave the facility a resort-like flavor. Surfing ranked high on the list of recreational activities. A dynamic staff, still bubbling with enthusiasm from launching a new adventure, made the Sunshine Academy a very desirable placement in the minds of parents and referral sources alike. The executive director had over fifteen years of experience in administering mental health programs for youth. The clinical director's doctorate degree spoke well of his training and experience. In all, the credentials of the clinical staff were impeccable. It was no surprise that the coed residential treatment center was full and had a waiting list for enrollment.

The therapeutic milieu was governed by a well-developed student handbook. It featured detailed rules and guidelines for prosocial conduct and spelled out consequences for maladaptive behaviors. Likewise, the manual described how a student council would be an integral part in shaping the rules of the road and providing input on a number of topics ranging from menu planning to recreational activities. The student handbook was reflective of a conscious effort for clients and staff to work together. It was indicative of the leadership's effort not to rule or reign with a heavy hand but to encourage active client participation throughout the treatment process.

One year into operations, the rate of client admissions declined—much to the puzzlement of the entire staff. A number of meetings were held to look for causality. Unable to put their fingers on possible reasons for sagging admission numbers, the administration looked for outside consulting help. The first hour of the consultant's campus visit was spent touring the various buildings in the company of some students. Posters of scantily clad women were noticed in the boy's dormitory along with a life-size image of Bob Marley—dreadlocks, cannabis-leaf-decorated shirt and all. The remainder of the day was spent interviewing clients. A concerning picture emerged. It was noticed that the students, advocating for themselves, were able to persuade the administration to make individual and group adaptations to milieu rules. As an example, John was able to negotiate a different bedtime from the other dorm mates. Mary, utilizing the power of the student council, was able to alter the one-piece-bathing-suit rule to permit the wearing of bikinis.

A subsequent interview with the clinical director revealed a strong commitment to flexibility. The consultant was lectured that creating a teenage-friendly environment must be based on adaptations, give-and-take, and compromise. Ruling with an iron fist would only engender opposition and defiance. This philosophy was well documented in bold letters on the first page of the student manual: "All Rules Are

Negotiable." The consultant concluded that the "flexibility doctrine" was not warmly embraced by parents and referral sources—the obvious smoking gun of the decline in admissions.

CONSIDERATIONS FOR SOLUTIONS

Creating a therapeutic milieu in which staff and clients work together toward a mutually agreed goal must be the aim of any facility. This task may encounter small and large hurdles when behavioral expectations differ between the caregiver and client. In most cases, it is the client that challenges the "rules of the road." Consequently, bringing about an optimal working relationship between staff and clients requires relationship-building skills. Striking the proper balance is not achieved by capitulating to every client demand nor holding on to a rule with an iron grip—and never, under any circumstance, considering any modification. The skill in administering a functional milieu lies in eliciting buy-in for nonnegotiable ground rules and finding the power to keep reasonable adaptations under control. Internal integrity in any therapeutic milieu is compromised when certain doors of maladaptive behaviors are not closed. Communicating to a group of adolescents that all rules are negotiable leaves every door ajar. Adolescents have a knack for slipping through half-open doors. Manipulating staff and other clients—and, in some cases, demanding to go through an open door—typically is not helpful in an environment that is charged with replacing maladaptive with prosocial behavior.

The Problem: The Trickle Effect of Green

The New Life Center, a residential treatment program for girls, was operating successfully for a number of years. Founded by clinicians, much attention was devoted to developing policies and procedures manuals.

Staff growth and development training had a large footprint. Manuals that provided operational clarity ranged from admission criteria to fire-drill procedures. Providing state-of-the-art patient care was foremost on the minds of founders and clinicians alike. Extensive years of employee service were celebrated with cash awards, extra days off, or stays at a vacation resort. Employees felt at home and connected with each other.

Approaching the age of retirement, the three owners of the center made a decision to sell the operation to a venture capitalist firm. In part, one of the conditions of the sale was based on having one of the owners continue as the executive director for two to three years. The continuation of the former leadership assured the continuation of the services. The rank and file of the employees were barely affected by the change in ownership. Their status quo was assured.

What did change was the job description of the executive director. New tasks like (a) creating an annual budget, (b) projecting client admissions and discharges, (c) projecting an average daily census for the coming year, (d) creating a detailed marketing plan, (e) projecting net earnings, and (f) submitting the monthly profit-and-loss statements were added to the to-do list. None of these tasks were unreasonable and, in fact, are the foundation of any well-run business.

Business as usual appeared assured. An aggressive approach to growing the business of the parent company changed all that. New programs, residential treatment centers, and therapeutic boarding schools were added in rapid succession. As most of the individual programs drew admission from the same referral sources, competition among the sister programs grew sharply. The net result was a decline in admission at New Life Center. This consequently put pressure on meeting the projected annual earnings target and, in turn, quadrupled the phone time between the corporate officer and the center's executive director. The new owners demanded a solution to the problem.

The ultimate outcome of these "pressure meetings" resulted in the corporate mandate to admit clients outside the established admission criteria for the treatment center. The behavioral and cognitive makeup of the newcomers had marked effects on the therapeutic milieu. The cohesiveness among the clients decreased, parents' questions regarding programmatic changes increased, referral sources launched grave concerns, and finally, the staff struggled to bring about optimal change in the daily administration of the milieu. All stakeholders of client improvement, including parents, clients, referral sources, and staff, knew that something had changed—and not for the better. It was not surprising that the leadership of the New Life Center expected a further decline in the average daily census.

CONSIDERATION OF SOLUTIONS

Maintaining an effective therapeutic community demands the attention of skilled staff—not just a skilled staff but a committed staff. No two days in the milieu are identical, as the interaction among clients and staff is not a carbon copy from day to day. Like an amoeba, the therapeutic community takes on different forms. Nonetheless, in order to maintain integrity and accountability, the staff is saddled with the challenge to keep the amoeba an amoeba and not let it mutate into some other creature.

Healthy and optimally operating programs strive to maintain integrity throughout the operation. Financial goals must be aligned with operational goals and policy. Yes, a business must be profitable. This raises the question, "Does profitability come through the trust and accountability generated from a solid commitment to clinical success or through the goal of filling beds at the cost of program integrity?" There are mortgages, expenses, and salaries to be paid. However, if outside referral sources and parents consider the program to be off center—a lightweight moneymaker—then the outcome of said program is doomed. It won't take much time for clients to feel they have been duped. Programmatic integrity should not be sacrificed at the altar of budgetary considerations. If census goals are no longer supporting financial targets, there are a number of remedies without compromising the fragile balance of a given therapeutic community. Initiating new services, finding separate space to accommodate a different client profile, and making changes in marketing and business development plans are just a few of a host of options that can preserve integrity throughout the organization.

Summary

Integrity and accountability are the foundations of an optimally functioning therapeutic community. They create predictability and security in both clients and staff. This trust is paramount to success. In the words of Zig Ziglar, "The most important persuasion tool you have in your entire arsenal is integrity. If people like you, they'll listen to you. But if they trust you, they'll do business with you." Because the milieu is a living organism, it can sometimes be squeezed from both internal and external sources. While the uncomfortable impact is inevitable, authentic dedication to the consistency of actions, values, methods, and principles helps keep a business in check. There is vision. There is knowledge of therapeutics. There is a core plan in motion with the intent of success. Whether deciding to keep the plan simple, keep the plan leading edge, or keep the plan rigorous and hardy—above all, keep the plan true. Leaders and employees must be committed to adhering to the vision set forth in mission statements and throughout all operational manuals, handbooks, and in-service training sessions.

CHAPTER 3

Cooking on All Burners

Maintaining an Optimal Measuring System of Progress
across the Different Stages of Change

JARED U. BALMER

I N A RESIDENTIAL SETTING, MEASURING THERAPEUTIC GAIN IS not restricted to individual, group, or family therapy. The therapeutic environment, or milieu, where the client spends most time is a significant tool for change. Properly conceived and administered, it serves as a measuring device for therapeutic gain. Therefore, program operators are challenged to create and maintain a milieu that not only facilitates change but also measures the progress of the target population.

The Problem: Underinflation

The staff of a new residential treatment facility spent considerable time drafting the outline of a therapeutic environment, or "rules of the road." A long list of rules delineated what behaviors were permitted, welcomed, and encouraged. Conversely, a list of out-of-bounds behaviors was established. In each case, the positive or negative consequences were addressed in association with each rule and guideline. Such guidelines and rules filled pages of paper. Delineation of the daily schedule, grooming and hygiene standards, and behaviors that provided the client with increased privileges and those that would result in sanctions were painstakingly addressed. More specifically, these program rules were tailored to the five phases or levels of progression build into the therapeutic milieu. Each level of progression was tied to advances in the change process, calling for increased demands, consistency, and privileges for each progressive stage. As each level is an indication of the continuing change process, clients were expected to work through all five levels of progression to complete the goals of the program. As an example, for a client to progress from level 2 to level 3, he had to be in compliance with 80 percent of all the rules over a period of up to two months. However, a breach of one of the core rules, like "no stealing," would land him on level 1—starting the climbing process from level to level all over again. The conglomeration of these rules was combined in a small booklet and given to each new client entering the program.

Some eight months into operations, several issues were noted by the staff. First, 70 percent of the client population were on levels 2 and 3. Fifteen percent of the population was on level 1, with the residual percentages on levels 4 and 5.

Percentage of Level Distribution among Client Population

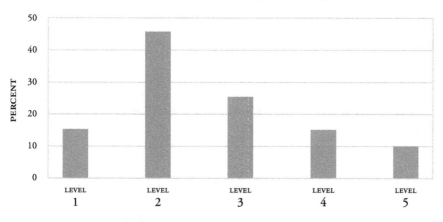

The staff lamented the dearth of leadership among the client population. Role modeling from those who fully embraced change was thinly spread throughout the therapeutic community. As staff members were cognizant that it was the first year of operation, the number of clients on level 1 was expected, as new admissions were arriving with relative frequency. However, a large segment of the client population became stagnant on level 2. The childcare staff complained that most of their time was consumed by clients on levels 1 and 2. The therapeutic community appears out of balance.

The Problem: Overinflation

A therapeutic boarding school has operated for several years. Similar to the previous example, the school measured student progress through a level system. Student improvement and performance were measured on effort and progression of therapy, education, recreation, and citizenship. The school operated on a rolling enrollment schedule, with students coming and leaving each month. Clients were expected to work through all five levels of progression. Because new students arrived monthly, there was always a small number of them on level 1. Yet they progressed rather quickly through the level system so that 75 percent of the students were distributed on levels 4 and 5, with only 20 percent of clients on levels 2 and 3.

Percentage of Level Distribution among Client Population

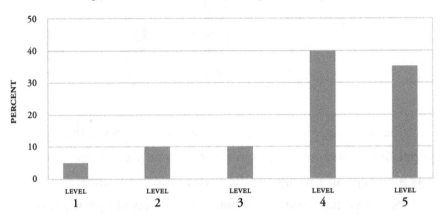

Over the past several months, the administration received an increasing number of calls from parents centered on the question, "My child has been on the highest level for a long time. Is it time for her to come home?" Faced with the fact that more and more parents pressured the school for the discharge dates of their children, the school leadership was pressed into a problem-solving meeting. They recognized that during the early years of operation, the distribution of students along the level system was heavily shaded to the lower levels. In an attempt to balance such distributions, the requirements for each level changed. The net result was a faster shifting of the student population to higher levels. However, when examining the question of "Are they ready for discharge?" the collective answer was "No." Now the school found itself in the regrettable and embarrassing position of having to explain to parents why their students, who had been on the highest level for six to eight months, were not ready for graduation.

Measuring Progress

Any group of individuals brought together with the aim of improving behavior is confronted with the question of how to measure progress. The nature of the presenting problems, the ages of the participants, the clinical complexity, and the average length of the treatment regimen are only some of the variables that are contributing factors for measuring progress. Virtually all models of behavioral change identify six stages. They are precontemplation, contemplation, determination, action, maintenance, and termination. These stages of change are fundamentally applicable in any setting. However, the measuring process becomes increasingly complex throughout the mental health continuum of care. In outpatient settings, where the individual participates in a weekly session with a therapist, measuring is relatively simple. As the length of treatment and therapeutic components are added, measuring progress increases in complexity. Adding to the base of individual therapy, additional services like group, family, milieu, recreational, and psychopharmacological therapy call for the evaluation of a wider range of outcome targets. Including an educational component in the form of an elementary, middle school, or high school curriculum as part of the program offering will further increase the complexity of measuring progress. As the measuring process increases in complexity, so does the need for each participant to understand the goal of the change process and identify thresholds of achievements along the way.

> As the measuring process increases in complexity, so does the need for each participant to understand the goal of the change process and identify thresholds of achievements along the way.

Traditional Level Systems

Traditional level systems are defined by evaluating the client on multiple variables concurrently in order to progress from one level to the next. The following example will demonstrate this issue:

A residential treatment program is offering individual, group, and family therapy along with robust adventure education, a prescriptive activity of daily living (ADL) program, and a fully accredited formal education curriculum. The facility also offers equine therapy and has a part-time medical staff that is responsible for physical health and the implementation of psychopharmacological therapy. The program has five levels. Each level has very specific target goals in all of the areas described above.

As previously stated, measuring all of such program offerings concurrently can become a very complex undertaking. The creation of such a system must take a host of guidelines, variables, and measuring methodologies into consideration. This may include the following:

- **Grooming standards.** Length of hair, appropriateness of clothing, etc.

- **Personal hygiene.** Showers, brushing of teeth, use of deodorant, handwashing, etc.

- **Rules of basic conduct.** No violence/harm again self and others, no stealing, no unauthorized absence from the program, etc.

- **Activities for daily living.** Adhering to a daily schedule, keeping personal space/bedroom organized, washing personal clothing and or bedding, demonstrating good table manners, participating in facility-wide cleaning and improvement projects, participating in levels of the program, etc.

- **Clinical treatment plan.** Participation in setting therapeutic goals and objectives, effort and follow-through with assignments, absence of treatment-interfering behavior, level of participation in individual, group, and family therapy, etc.)

- **Recreation and diversionary activity.** Level of participation, care of equipment, willingness to try new things, following safety rules and guidelines, etc.)

- **Formal classroom education.** Following general classroom rules, effort, focus, follow-through, level of participation, interaction with classmates, etc.)

- **Equine component.** Level of involvement/participation, grooming of horse, proper use of equipment, etc.

- **Medication.** Compliance, level of self-direction, etc.

Having identified all the measuring components, the program administrators are now confronted with additional critical tasks that will have long-range implications for the client population. They may include:

- **Defining an optimal threshold of progression between five levels.** What specifically is required for a client to qualify to move through all five levels for each of the identified program components? For example: What are the specific behaviors that are required from a client with regard to ADL?

- **Optimal separation of the levels.** Is there enough separation between requirements and expectations for all program elements across all five levels? Are the rewards and privileges for each level attractive enough to engender motivation for the next level? If such separation is minimal, what is the likelihood for a given client to simply be content "parking" himself or herself on a lower level?

- **Assigning weight to each component.** In the evaluation process of moving a client across the levels system, should one program component count more than another component? For example, is meeting the threshold for formal therapy more important than meeting the measure for recreation and diversionary activity? Is repeatedly forgetting to brush his teeth keeping a client from progressing to the next level, even though that client has demonstrated behaviors consistent with level 4 behavior in the clinical treatment area?

- **Graduation requirements.** When is a client ready to complete the program? Is the client required to achieve the highest level? If so, for how long? If the program graduates a client on level 3, what message is being sent to the rest of the client population?

- **Decision-making.** Who are the evaluators of progression for a given client? Which staff members make that decision? How much objectivity or subjectivity comes into play to make that decision? Does a certain client have "darling" status and is favored over others? If there are split opinions, who has the final say? Should the childcare staff override the opinion of the primary therapist of a given client? If so, when?

Any organization hoping to implement a traditional level system must give careful consideration to these questions. Failure to do so will result in a rapid, ever-changing, and moving target with respect to measuring therapeutic progression. This may have disturbing effects on the client population. That is not to say that adjustments are inappropriate. As anyone who ever operates a level system will know, clients are quick to find loopholes. In such cases, the level creators must determine when any adjustments are in line with the mission statement of the facility.

POTENTIAL PITFALLS OF TRADITIONAL LEVEL SYSTEMS

Any measuring tool designed to evaluate behavior can encounter potential problems. Evaluating human behavior always carries with it a certain degree of subjectivity. That subjectivity is influenced by what is being measured, the subject under evaluation, and who is doing the observation. Unless one is counting narrowly defined behaviors by specifically trained observers, it remains inevitable that partiality and objective difficulties may arise. Within a host of client variables, finding complete agreement among a number of observers is not a given. To achieve complete inter-rater reliability is a goal that is not routinely achieved. This phenomenon has direct implications in administering a level system. Here are some obvious pitfalls:

Slam-Dunking

Consider the following situation: Max has been enrolled in a residential treatment center for six months. On the program's level system, he achieved a level 4 out of 5 but has remained stagnant there much longer than expected. While Max has demonstrated regular level 4 behavior, he has stubbornly failed to do what is required for level 5. The clinical director called a staff meeting to discuss what should be done. It was determined that Max was perfectly capable of achieving the needed comportment to jump to level 5. The conclusion was that he was simply stubborn. Though not egregious, this maladaptive behavior kept him from progressing. The frustrated staff wanted to teach him a lesson. As a result, Max was placed on level 1. He was told that he would stay there until he gave up his stubbornness and engaged in behavior consistent with level 5 guidelines.

Slam-dunking is related to a number of problems that have negative effects on the entire treatment community:

1. The level system has been altered for a single student.

2. Max, who did show consistent level 4 behavior, will likely see this demotion as unfair punishment. Conversely, his alleged stubbornness may erupt into retaliatory behavior.

3. His friends may come to his defense, questioning the staff about their own rules and possibly contributing to an uproar in the milieu.

4. Inevitably, such demotions will come to the attention of Max's parents or professional referral sources. This may trigger a cascade of questions and send staff scrambling to find adequate answers, with a net effect of calling the integrity of the program into question.

5. Setting a precedent of slam-dunking could trigger copycat behavior among the staff, with system-wide destructive results.

Slam-dunking is a pitfall of any level system. Its routine practice is not only unethical but also is a possible death sentence for any respected treatment facility utilizing a traditional level system. Routine slam-dunking will lead to the underinflation of the level system (see above), with the majority of clients parked on the lower levels without the leadership of highly motivated peers capable of leading by example. There are a host of other options available to get Max unstuck from his level 4 perch—all predicated on Max staying at level 4 while the applied intervention is being implemented.

Bar-Raising the Second Time Around

Consider the following scenario, which is the close cousin of slam-dunking:

Meg, an eighteen-year-old young woman, has been at a young adult transition program for five months. Prior to her admission, she successfully completed a fourteen-month-long program in which she was treated for reactive attachment disorder (RAD). There, it was determined a stay at a transitional living program would boost her ability to live independently while attending a junior college. The milieu of the young adult program operated in three houses. Clients would move from the investment through the maintenance and eventually to the transition house as part of the therapeutic journey. Meg progressed through both the investment and the maintenance houses and had been at the transition house for three months when, for reasons unknown, she stole money from a fellow roommate—a behavior never observed at the maintenance house. At a multidisciplinary staff meeting, it was determined that Meg should return back to the maintenance house, as her maladaptive behavior was not in keeping with the transition house guidelines. It became clear that Meg had not fully internalized the changes required to warrant the progression to the next treatment phase. In order to "guarantee" such internalization, Meg was told that for her specifically, the threshold of behavioral expectations at the maintenance house would be raised. In essence, she understood that getting to the transition house the second time around would be harder.

The pitfalls of raising the bar the second time around share many of the same problems associated with slam-dunking. In most cases it is not a smart therapeutic intervention. This is particularly true in that Meg's stealing occurrence was never a prior behavior. Like Max, Meg inevitably will interpret such intervention as harsh and unacceptable, which may trigger impulses to check herself out of the program. Dealing with these issues at the current transition phase in Meg's journey will prove far more beneficial and will likely decrease the chance of negative fallout from Meg, her parents, and other stakeholders.

Golfers Have Handicaps

Consider the following: a residential treatment center has admitted four new students within a given month. One of the students came directly from home. His previous treatment history included one year of weekly individual therapy in an outpatient setting. The second student had a minor involvement with the law and consequently was sent to an outdoor behavioral health program prior to her admission. The third student had a history of multiple short-term psychiatric hospitalizations prior to his admission. The fourth student had been seen by a host of outpatient clinicians over a period of eight years.

The relative variability of the mental health and treatment history of these clients begs the question of whether or not each should begin his or her treatment program from the same starting line. Golfers measure their achievements on a given golf course by taking into account their individual handicaps. Would such an approach be advisable in this case? Any treatment program making full use of a traditional level system must answer such questions if they want to cook on all burners—making full and optimal use of the level system. Overlooking such questions may give rise to a chorus of complaints from the client population of "You are not treating me fairly." This can look discouraging, even to kids who are progressing well on the level system. Such sentiments may also instigate an escalation in a program's negative "underground" (addressed in chapter 6) with ruinous effects, up to and including the death of a treatment program. On the other hand, beginning from the same starting line is possible, depending on how the level creators structure the measuring stick, taking into account that not all clients are the same. Thought should be given to individual differences.

Concrete versus Ethereal Level Progression

Consider the following: In a comprehensive treatment center, the multidisciplinary staff reviews each client on a monthly basis to determine the readiness for level progression. The client's effort, compliance with rules, participation, involvement, work, accomplishments, setbacks, etc., are reviewed. Based on the given level criteria, a certain client is reviewed and found not eligible to progress, yet the direct staff supervisor says, "I feel like the student deserves the next level." Such ethereal or "I have a feeling" decisions can take on many forms, including but not limited to: "He has reached level 3 way too fast. We are going to make it harder for him to reach the next level or, she screwed up on her last home visit. We are going to have to change the rules for her on the next visit."

In the realm of human behavior, there are always concrete and subjective decision-making processes. No level system, regardless of minutiae and precision, is going to do away with subjectivity altogether. However, when subjectivity is pushing too hard on the well-established rules, the integrity of the program structure is compromised. Case in point: On a consulting visit to a residential treatment program, the author of this chapter reviewed the student handbook. On the first page, in bold letters, was the declaration that "All rules are negotiable." Sadly, the clinical team had fallen prey to the misconception that individuality, in all or its manifestations, supersedes basic rules of human interaction at any time. This mindset resulted in the program's short life span.

Trapped in the Dogma

Consider the following: a therapeutic boarding school accepted two new students on the same date. Jeff, a seventeen-year-old, had an expensive history of drug and alcohol abuse, for which he was treated in a substance-abuse rehabilitation center prior to his admission. Paul, a fourteen-year-old, was admitted for an extensive history of school refusal. He had no history of substance abuse. During a school outing, Jeff was able to steal a can of beer from a convenience store and subsequently persuaded Paul to take a couple of sips. The student handbook was very explicit that any form of alcohol consumption carried with it an automatic loss of certain privileges. The administration, intent on upholding the integrity of the school, decided both students should lose the privileges defined by the rules.

The underlying history and the reasoning for the rules violation were fundamentally different for the two students. Yet the dogmatic application of the written rule failed to take into account individual differences and tailored consequences. A well-balanced level system that is designed to measure therapeutic progression must take into account the maturity levels and the behavioral histories of its clients. Such differences are best delineated in the student handbook, avoiding or at least minimizing the answer to the ever-present question of "Is that fair?"

Measuring Compliance versus Treatment Objectives

Consider the following: a residential treatment program is providing every student with a student handbook. The handbook is twelve pages long, double sided. Programmatic rules are addressed in great depth and may include:

- Daily hygiene

- Grooming

- Core safety rules

- General behavior in different environments such as the classroom or transpiration in cars

- Respect of property

- Peer interaction and relationships

- Taking care of bedding

- Organization of personal storage space

- Clothing reequipment and guidelines

- The wearing of artifacts (necklaces, earrings, etc.)

- Off-campus rules and behavior, home visits, use of radio or other electronic equipment, personal and room searches, and more

Virtually all these rules and guidelines are making their way into the level system, with the aim of defining level progression for both clients and the staff alike. The progress of each client is evaluated in monthly staff meetings attended by the clinical director, primary therapist, program director, childcare staff member, recreational and medical staff, nurse, and a classroom/teaching staff member. The ensuing discussion is primarily focused on whether or not, or to what degree, a given client demonstrates compliance to the above rules and guidelines.

The pitfalls of such a review process are primarily based on compliance at the expense of the evaluation of a few specific treatment objectives delineated in the client's master treatment plan. Such a review process can fall into the trap of favoring toothbrushing over mood elevation or refusing to complete a school assignment over purging food after each meal. The hyperattention to compliance may well be indicated for a client with oppositional tendencies, either as a core diagnosis or as a treatment-interfering behavior. However, "riding the compliance train" bound for a goal, without consideration of the individual components of the client, contributes to treatment failure for those who suffer from debilitating issues not based on compliance.

> Implementing and maintaining a well-balanced traditional level system pays equal attention to both core treatment goals and objectives and the maintenance of programmatic integrity.

Implementing and maintaining a well-balanced traditional level system pays equal attention to both core treatment goals and objectives and the maintenance of programmatic integrity.

Nontraditional Level Measuring Systems

Traditional level systems are defined by requiring that all elements of programing meet the highest level in order to achieve successful completion of the program. Though mentioned many times, it is worth repeating—to administer such a level system is a complex and often difficult task. Accounting for differences in age and maturity, behavioral and cognitive histories, along with the relative acuity of the presenting problems, can challenge the most accomplished creator of a therapeutic milieu. Depending on the demographics of the client population, an infinite assortment for measuring therapeutic progression can be utilized—only to be limited by the relative creativity of those so challenged. Such challenges may be mitigated as an increasing number of therapeutic delivery systems, ranging from outpatient to residential and inpatient care, become more specialized. Programing for a narrower band of mental disorders may be less complex than creating a program in which one size fits all. Consequently, a traditional system may undergo significant changes and adaptations more tailored to meet the underlying philosophy of change and the client population. Such models of measuring the therapeutic process can take on an infinite number of variations. Here are a few examples:

THE HIGH SCHOOL MODEL

Consider the following: Graduation from high school is, first and foremost, contingent on completing the required credit hours. Beyond this core measure of achievement is the consideration of the GPA—an indication of how well the student mastered the given subject matter. Another variable added to the completion of credit hours and GPA is citizenship. Less acceptable behavior like being tardy to class, having unexcused absences, etc., may present hurdles for the student but fall short of being dismissed from the school altogether. In essence, as long as the student passes all of the required classes in the program's matriculation, less-than-stellar citizenship behavior will not impede his graduation. While there is a minimal interplay between graduation requirement and citizenship behavior, accumulating the requirement of credit hours is the measure for success.

Following this model, a measuring system for therapeutic gain is, first and foremost, tied to the master treatment plan with its long- and short-term goals and objectives. Whether the client is late for breakfast, does not tie his shoes, or fails to brush his teeth has no bearing on the long-term treatment goals of the individual. In this model, expectations of good citizenship are expected but bear little or no weight in determining whether the presenting problem has been resolved. For example, in a residential treatment center designed to treat eating disorders, proper folding of clothing items and bed making is not a critical determinant for therapeutic improvement. However, treating the bulimic behavior of purging food after meals is an essential component of the master treatment plan. In this system, a citizenship code exists. It addresses the prosocial behavior among its clients but does not indicate when treatment goals have been achieved.

Citizenship in this model addresses the need for guidelines that govern the daily interaction of the client population—basic expectations of civil behavior. Following such expectations can be rewarded with certain privileges (e.g., movie nights, outings, extra free time, etc.). Conversely, major infractions may carry with them appropriate consequences. The client will graduate from the program when the goals and objectives of the treatment plan are met, regardless of citizenship status.

POSITIVE PEER MODELS

Consider the following: the staff discovered that Gary, a seventeen-year-old client, was missing from campus. After an extensive search, Gary was found five miles away from campus. After a lengthy interaction with staff, he agreed to return to the program. Upon his return, a group of peers was assembled who confronted Gary about his unauthorized absence. Moreover, under the guidance of the staff group leader, the group of peers discussed what fitting consequences would need to be assigned to Gary.

While there are variations of the positive peer model that borrow from other milieu systems, a core element rests on the notion that peers often have a greater capacity of influence over the behavior of other peers as opposed to adults. In this model, a client's capacity to confront maladaptive behavior and provide positive feedback to group members is critical. Such behavior is often labeled as displaying great leadership. Consequently, one must demonstrate such leadership skills as part of the measuring process of achieving the desired treatment goals. Therefore, the dynamics, tenacity, and ability to influence peers become important measuring sticks in the treatment evaluation process. Skilled childcare staff utilizing this model are keenly aware that not all clients manifest their leadership skills with the same bravado. They recognize that quiet leadership can be just as impactful on peer behavior. Failure to recognize such quiet leadership leaves a timid or depressed client, or one with low self-esteem, underserved.

FAMILY TEACHING MODEL

Consider the following: let us borrow the same "Gary" from the positive peer model described above. Upon Gary's return to the program following his unauthorized escape, the family teaching model would intervene differently. Gary will be meeting with the staff alone. No other peers are present. In a neutral tone of voice, the staff member will elicit Gary's expiation of his runaway attempt. Gary's explanation is that he got very angry with a peer and "couldn't take it any longer." The staff person, acknowledging Gary's explanation and continuing in a neutral tone of voice—avoiding all verbal and nonverbal messages of anger or chastisement—is explaining to Gary all the maladaptive consequences of running away. The staff member explains to Gary that he needs to learn or strengthen certain skills—in this case, anger management. He is given a card that he carries with him on a daily basis. The card clearly states his goal of acquiring the proficiencies of anger management. Gary is encouraged to focus on this particular skill development for one month. When staff members observe him demonstrating this skill, he will receive verbal reinforcement along with a certain number of points. Conversely, anger outbursts will result in a loss of points.

In this model, skill development takes center stage. Therapeutic progression is not based on specific goals and objectives derived from a *DSM* diagnosis. It is all about prosocial skill development. Since individual therapy is typically restricted to one to two hours per week, the teaching of fundamental prosocial skills takes place during all waking hours. Therefore, the milieu is carrying the lion's share of the reasonability for the change process. The measuring of therapeutic progression is akin to a token-economy system whereby outcome is measured by the accumulation of points.

THE PURE ACCEPTANCE/RELATIONSHIP MODEL

Consider the following: Justin has been placed in an outdoor behavioral program. At sixteen years of age, he was expelled from the boarding school he attended for selling drug paraphernalia. Concurrently, Justin's behavior at home has increasingly contributed to family conflict. Frequently violating curfew, stealing money from family members, and using verbal aggression all contributed to family chaos. Justin's refusal to participate in family therapy propelled the parents to send him to a wilderness program.

After a thorough search for any drugs or drug paraphernalia by the intake staff and outfitting him with the necessary gear, he was taken out in the woods, where Justin joined a small group of peers. There, he was greeted by the staff overseeing the peers. Inquiring of staff members as to what he needed to do, the staff explained that the overall goal is to abandon maladaptive behavior in favor of practicing and embracing prosocial behavior. Within the general framework, Justin was encouraged and supported to develop his own goals and his own pace. Virtually all of the shaping of prosocial behavior came about by a combination of individual and group therapy, daily community groups, and appropriate modeling by staff and peers. There was no specific target behavior attached to a level system. Only progression toward mutually agreed-upon goals was celebrated, and maladaptive behavior was processed through individual and group therapy and staff-led community groups.

In this model, a traditional level system is completely abandoned, and so are any therapeutic thresholds of progressions attached to specific sanctions or privileges. The measurement for progression in treatment is not based on incremental steps but determined by arriving at the end target goal. The model is designed for the client to engage in prosocial behavior for intrinsic reasons, not motivated by external privileges and rewards. The tools for shaping prosocial behavior in the client are primarily based on modeling by staff and the peers who have embraced changed behavior. Such progression is celebrated with positive reinforcement. Such reinforcements are, first and foremost, based on the hopes of organic changes in the client, not by extrinsic tokens.

Summary

Formal individual, group, and family therapy comprises a small amount of the time spent in a residential treatment setting. Of the 112 waking hours in a given week, typically, no more than 10 hours are spent in formal therapy with a licensed clinician. Indeed, the therapeutic milieu is a major contributing factor to the change process. Its creation and maintenance can never be underestimated. A "therapeutic" milieu must (a) capture the seminal aspects of the presenting problems of the client, and (b) be optimally weighted across the client population by taking full advantage of those clients who demonstrate therapeutic progression and therefore serve as role models.

Need for Complexity in Level/Measuring System

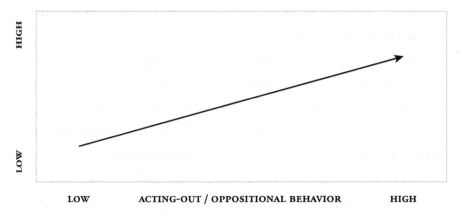

Serving a client population with an abundance of acting-out problems, in which deception and aggression occur with relatively high frequency, calls for a more complex milieu that addresses such maladaptive behaviors in greater detail. Conversely, holding a client with social panic disorder back from level advancement because he or she fails to make a bed appropriately is counterproductive. The measuring process of the therapeutic milieu has to be closely tied to the symptomatology of the client population. In general terms, the necessity for the increased complexity and articulation of behaviors in the milieu increases with the acting-out or oppositional behavior of the population served.

CHAPTER 4

Weather Forecasting

*Anticipating Situations in Which the Culture Is Most
Vulnerable for Negative Influence and Deterioration*

W. KIMBALL DELAMARE

WEATHER FORECASTING REFERS TO THE ABILITY OF the caregivers to leverage their knowledge to manage potential difficulty in "climatic" patterns within the client population. Such weather changes are often predictable and are related to a variety of circumstances. By predicting and preparing for such disturbing patterns, staff members can prevent a temporary rainstorm or possibly a long-term climate change.

The Problem: Low Tide

At the Maryland Mountain Retreat Center, Eliza, the residential staff supervisor, was conducting her annual safety survey by reviewing incident reports. She noted that most incidents took place on weekends, evenings, and Friday afternoons. These times corresponded to when many of the professional staff members, such as teachers and therapists, were not on campus. It also represented a time on the weekly schedule typically less busy with activities including school and formal group therapy—a laxer or "low tide" period. In an effort to reduce the number of incidents, Eliza approached the administration with the suggestion of increasing the staff coverage during these times. The feedback was not what she hoped for.

Having remained on campus to conduct telephone family therapy at least two evenings each week, the therapist eagerly anticipated an early departure on Friday afternoon. Likewise, the teachers finished their last class periods at 3:00 p.m. and looked forward to the weekend. The low-tide issue was compounded by two problems. First, the most senior childcare workers were scheduled during the morning and early afternoon, leaving the least experienced staff to manage the milieu during a laxer time of the day and weekend. Second, Eliza found it difficult to summon backup staff when the "weather clouds moved in." It was inevitable that most of the incident reports showed up on Eliza's desk on a Monday morning.

The Problem: Borrow from Peter to Pay Paul

Tom, a human resources director, dreaded certain months during the year. First, he was charged with massive paperwork associated with the annual performance reviews of over eighty employees. Concurrently, annual health insurance renewal, adjustment, and sign-up demanded much of his time, far beyond his regular workload. On the heels of such time demands, Thomas would groan as he considered the significant staff turnover during the summer months. Such turnover was fueled by current employees embarking on graduate school or restarting their college dreams.

Tom's plea for extra help during this time rendered two responses from the administration. He was reminded that during the normal time of the year, his workload was routine and manageable. The current higher workload was short lived. In an attempt to help remedy Tom's stress (distress), the administration offered the help of a childcare worker, which in turn elicited a cry for help from the supervisor of the childcare staff.

The Problem: Santa Claus Is Coming

The Timber Range Center had been operating with many of the same employees since it opened eight years ago. Every year as the holidays approached, a debate ensued among the professional treatment staff as to which of them would be on call, responding to the emerging clinical and psychosocial needs of clients. As a sign of some sort of initiation to the center, the newest member of the therapy staff was tagged for this assignment. The exception to this routine was a staff member who lived in close proximity to the treatment facility. A suggestion that every other year, the executive director may want to volunteer for the Christmas shift fell on unfruitful soil. The reason "I can never get away from work" was reiterated. Intermittently, other solutions were tried to reduce the workload on the staff in general and the on-call clinician in particular. Solutions like extending the leave of absence for clients, on-call minishifts for professional staff, less structure and more "fun time" for those clients remaining on campus were implemented—with some, but limited, success. The problem of staffing for holiday times remained and gave rise to gathering clouds in the milieu.

CONSIDERATIONS FOR SOLUTIONS

Each of these problems finds its origin in the leadership of the organization and has the potential to rain on the parade of the client therapeutic milieu. These weather patterns do not require an advanced degree in meteorology. Not only are they predictable and obvious, but they are also relatively easy to prevent. Spacing high-intensity workloads like annual performance evaluations across the entire year, thereby avoiding processing many employees within a short timeframe, is an easier and more manageable solution. Increasing the staff-to-student ratio over less structured time throughout the day or week is simply good practice and has a positive effect on the governance and supervision of the therapeutic environment. In most organizations, entry-level positions experience the highest turnover rates. Lack of upward mobility and the pursuit of further educational goals are among the chief reasons for seasonal turnover. Hiring and staffing will always be ongoing issues, but companies shouldn't be caught in a surprise cloudburst without an umbrella. Knowing an organization's employee turnover pattern helps predict the hiring process. Such foreknowledge allows the administration to be proactive instead of scrambling for solutions after the departure of staff members.

> Adding staff or financial resources is often insufficient to bring about the desired outcome. Such situations call for creative, well-trained staff to dispel the gathering clouds.

Less Predictable Weather Patterns

Not all problems are as obvious as the ones identified above. There are issues that require a closer examination to find a solution. Moreover, adding staff or financial resources is often insufficient to bring about the desired outcome. Such situations call for creative, well-trained staff to dispel the gathering clouds. There are no shortages in anticipating problem situations. Below are a few examples.

The Problem: Where Are the Leaders?

The Hilltop Academy is a therapeutic boarding school with rolling enrollment. New entries and graduations of students from the school may take place monthly. The student body consisted of more than sixty-five residents. Spring had arrived at the Hilltop Academy, and students anticipated the upcoming spring break with excitement. Those who had been in the program for longer than six months were eligible to leave the academy for home visits. Those who stayed behind were newer students who had not earned the privilege and also a couple of clients whose behavior was clinically contraindicated for successful home visits.

It did not take long for a malaise to sweep over the student population. In some cases, disappointment was transformed into anger. From the kids, phrases like "Shut up"; "Get lost"; and "Who are you to tell me what to do?" spread through campus and were directed at each other but also toward the staff. It became obvious that the more established students—those who were group catalysts for greater behavioral maturity—were missing. The absence of their positive influence and prosocial modeling had a negative effect on the peers who remained on campus. It would not be an overstatement to say the remaining clients in the milieu were caught in seasonal turbulence.

CONSIDERATIONS FOR SOLUTIONS

Any therapeutic group of individuals has leaders. Some are formally designated as such. Others simply emerge through their prosocial behavior. When those leaders are absent for an extended time, shifts in group dynamics are inevitable. A shift may progress into toxicity fueled by one or two outspoken, angry clients. In this situation, the staff can employ a number of strategies to intervene and bring about a positive change.

- **Recruit new leaders.** The absence of established student leaders may provide a window for recruiting new leaders. Such a strategy involves the identification of a small group of clients—students who may not be perfect but who show progress and will not shy away from modeling prosocial behavior. Could these students be induced to prove their individual therapeutic progress by demonstrating leadership qualities? Perhaps they receive an invitation to a special, private meeting in which the staff defines the problem and asks for their help in solving it. Such a recruitment process may be associated with the promise of primary or secondary reinforcers. In addition, encouragements like "You have progressed to this maturity level; otherwise, we would not invite you to attend this meeting" may provide the motivation to demonstrate leadership behavior. Moreover, such students can be celebrated in the presence of the other peers for showing significant growth.

- **Divide and conquer.** It is easier to manage a small, as opposed to a larger, group. Even a small group of toxic students is dealt with more successfully than attempting the task within the context of a large peer group. Clients who display maladaptive behavior demand the negative attention of the whole group. They thrive on it. (For an in-depth discussion of intervening with such students, see chapter 5.) Breaking up the larger group into small groups can take on different forms. All groups may be challenged to complete a task, with the winning group being rewarded with a pizza party or an untold number of primary or secondary reinforcers. Other formats may include a diverse group task in a round-robin situation. One group could go on a day hike, another group to visit a museum, etc. The options are endless. Conversely, suggesting activities that are interpreted as "work" are readily labeled as punishment and should be avoided.

The Problem: Too Much of a Good Thing

The New Life Residential Treatment Center, like many other such facilities, experienced a seasonal drop and rise in the monthly census of enrollment. During the early summer months, the center would lose up to one-half of its students to graduation. Such a change was fueled by parents anxious to bring their adolescents home in anticipation of starting the new school year in their home communities. For the center's therapeutic milieu, this meant that the most improved students were absent and no longer in a position to provide prosocial modeling for their newer peers. In short, much of the leadership of the student community was gone. The second issue in this yearly scenario was the negative financial effect. Faced with an unfavorable bottom line, the administration put pressure on the admissions department to fill the empty beds in short order. As a result, a relatively large number of new students was admitted during a short time period. Most of the new admits met the admission criteria. However, the urgency to fill beds compromised the vetting process for a few individuals who were on the borders of the admission criteria. Regardless, the administration was thrilled with the quick recovery. It was a good thing ... maybe.

Admitting a large number of students during a short time span changed the dynamics of the therapeutic milieu. During the honeymoon period—a time when new students observe the lay of the land—no significant changes were noted. However, after a while the climate in the milieu heated up as some of the new enrollees began to test the behavioral boundaries of the program. With all staff hands on deck, it still took months to rectify the milieu.

CONSIDERATIONS FOR SOLUTIONS

Bringing in a large group of new clients is challenging. It will test the know-how of the staff, whether an organization is starting a new program or is faced with this issue midstream. Fundamentally, the approach of creating or restoring a functional milieu lies in the art of team building. Volumes of books have been written about team-building activities, most of which are directed toward business enterprises, not for mental health endeavors. Regardless of the target audience, many of these team-building activities have relevance and can easily be adapted to treatment settings. Before we mention some options, it might be good to go over what is accomplished during these activities. The benefits include:

- Improvement in communication skills

- Increased morale and patience

- Greater confidence individually and as a group

- The opportunity to see rising leadership skills

- Bonding with staff

- Increased effectiveness and cohesion within the group

Effective team-building activities for adolescents and young adults have adventurous and challenging components. Ropes-course obstacles, in which groups of individuals are challenged to problem solve, are very effective. These activities combine mental or physical challenges, fun, and adventure and are highly engaging. Access to a commercial ropes course is not required. Many of these activities can be set up within a building or outdoors. Frankly, team building doesn't always need to be adventurous. Challenges come in various ways that can build team spirit. We perused the bookstore and the internet for ideas.

- Geocaching in teams

- Forehead Dots

- Human Knots

- Spaghetti Tower

- Flip This Sheet Challenge

- Good works volunteering

The list goes on ... and on. Paramount for team building is the need to process these activities through the group, with the emphasis of working together to meet the stated challenge.

The Problem: The Long and Short of It

The We-Can-Help-You treatment program had a coed student body of forty clients. They ranged in ages between fourteen and eighteen. Financial sources for the tuition were a mixed bag. Some parents paid cash. For other clients, funding came from insurance companies and third-party payer sources. As the organization's ability to provide charity care was limited, the clinical team produced initialized treatment plans based on the projected length of stay for a given student. Since the length of stay in part was determined by the funding, a wide range in length of stay was standard practice for the center. This created a schism of sorts within the therapeutic milieu. Clients with the means for longer stays resented the early departures of those with shorter stay resources. Some students with shorter stays taunted those with longer stays. Explanations by the staff that each person's stay was based on different measuring sticks did not wash with many longer-term students. Overtly and covertly, such sentiments were woven into the fabric of the client community. Correspondingly, the staff was saddled with dealing with these issues time and time again.

CONSIDERATIONS FOR SOLUTIONS

To operate a treatment program for students with a wide range of time constraints is riddled with problems. Such problems pervade the entire organization and affect all service areas. Inevitably, it is the clients and those charged with the day-to-day supervision who are most burdened with this issue. It is an ongoing challenge that is hard to overcome. The only effective way to approach the dilemma is to separate the short-termers from the long-termers. This can be done in a variety of ways. They can be housed in separated dormitories or kept under the same roof but with separate assigned quarters. Equally important is that the student handbook—the rules of the road—must have a different focus for the two groups. Overlaps are inevitable and necessary, but the purpose, aim, and desired outcome must be stated to match the general treatment plan of two distinct populations.

The Problem: The Star Is Leaving

Teri was one of those amazing staff members. As the supervisor of the childcare staff, she enjoyed the admiration and support from both her subordinates and clients alike. Dealing with students who were upset or had temporarily slipped into a funk was her forte. In many ways, Teri was the glue that held the therapeutic community together. After being accepted to the graduate program at a local university, she terminated her employment with the organization. Understandably, everyone who worked with her was sad. Over the ensuing weeks, several incidents emerged.

- Two students slated for discharge in the near future demonstrated signs of regression. One boy showed increased opposition, and a young girl was often found in tears.

- One student, on a home visit the day Teri left, refused to come back to the program. He had bonded with her to the degree that "nobody else" was able to replace her.

- Another student sabotaged her upcoming home visit. She felt that Teri was instrumental in helping her prepare for the leave of absence. Now that Teri was gone, the girl felt she lacked the moral support to meet the challenges of leaving the program—even for a short home visit.

- Many of the childcare workers were underimpressed with Teri's replacement. Some of the watercooler talk implied the hiring of her replacement was a mistake.

- Both therapists and teachers were equally unhappy. They expressed dismay with the new lack of communication between the three service areas (the milieu, education, and therapy). According to them, information and directives of the professional staff no longer consistently made it to the therapeutic milieu and its staff members.

Teri's departure had a wide and long impact on the entire facility—all that anyone could see were dark clouds on the horizon. Employees and clients had been working through the fallout for weeks.

CONSIDERATIONS FOR SOLUTIONS

Overcoming the departure of a key employee is never an easy task. An individual who has created a high standard of performance is not easily recreated overnight. While we want to hang on to every good worker in our businesses, permanency in any position within the organization is not a given. However, proactive measures can be implemented to mitigate this issue. Considering the client reaction in the above case, it is not clinically prudent to have an exclusive connection with a given staff member. Of course, it is natural for certain clients to relate better to certain staff members. However, clients need to respect and have a connection with all caregivers. A client who is exclusively connected with a single therapeutic staff member often fails to take the broader view of newly learned prosocial behavior and attitudes into a setting outside the treatment environment. In that regard, multiple staff members must take the time to create a comfortable one-on-one relationship with a given student—minus exclusivity.

On the administrative side of the equation, program leaders must always be on the lookout for the replacement of key employees. The most expeditious way of filling a vacancy is from within the company. We know—it is not always possible. But as we will discuss in chapter 7, it is good to cross-train and find ways within the organization to bolster the expertise of people with whom you are already familiar, and then you are halfway there. Such an employee is typically demonstrating the skills and behavior that make for an easier transition. On the other hand, a replacement from outside the company involves a more in-depth vetting process. Is there energy? Do they seem comfortable in the adolescent setting? Can they take the heat of the job? In terms of the watercooler quarterbacking in any organization, people can be found who have taken fault finding to an advanced level. It behooves the administration to take the high road in these issues and find supportive ways to deal with complaining: "What would you suggest?" or "How would you deal differently with the problem you saw?"

The Problem: Finding the Sweet Spot of Diversity

The Venus Star Residential Treatment Center cast a wide admission net. The program was coed and ranged in ages from twelve to eighteen years. Their treatment philosophy was loosely based on the family teaching model. Such a model makes use of helping the clients negotiate developmental milestones with age-appropriate, prosocial behavior—the main strategy for the change process. To assist the facility in this approach, token-economy elements were employed. Individual target behaviors were marked by assigning points, which in turn could be redeemed in the form of status advancements. Such advancements were associated with increased rewards and privileges. This version of the family teaching model was augmented by providing a single weekly session of psychotherapy for each client.

Identifying the presenting problems of each client according to the *Diagnostic Statistical Manual* (*DSM*) rendered a wide variety of formal diagnoses. Depression, ADHD, oppositional defiant disorder, bipolar disorder, reactive attachment disorder, and anxiety disorders in all their variety were a major part of the list of client issues. A few outliers in the form of gender dysphoria, autism spectrum disorder, and addictive disorders were also represented.

The treatment environment was grounded on two platforms: formal therapies based on the diagnoses, as well as milieu progression via token economy for prosocial skill development. For many staff members, this hand-in-hand approach appeared optimal. Dealing with internal thought processes while concurrently shaping external behavior is the mental health version of killing two birds with one stone. Some clinicians, however, were not so sure this arrangement was the best approach. They felt that one hour of individual therapy was not enough to identify internal processes and provide specific treatment for them. Their concern was based on the fact that best practice models for different diagnoses called for homework with follow-up on assignments and practice outside the formal therapy session. The milieu was long on providing the platform for presenting prosocial behavior but short on providing the homework environment for some clients. The teaching model was ideal for the boy who suffered from oppositional behavior disorder but did little for the girl who suffered from depression because of a traumatic event at a younger age.

CONSIDERATIONS FOR SOLUTIONS

Creating an optimal treatment environment for a wide variety of clients with different diagnoses can inspire head scratching. The one-size-fits-all approach is not the answer for each client; while it serves some individuals well, others are underserved. In order to focus more specifically on individual problems that go beyond prosocial behavior, two options should be considered:

- Small groups of clients can be grouped together to address specific issues relative to their presenting diagnostic issues and closely related problems. Ideally, these groups are led by professional staff who are competent and trained in the group's respective special needs. A small sampling of specialty groups might have a focus on chemical abuse or dependency, anxiety-related

> The one-size-fits-all approach is not the answer for each client; while it serves some individuals well, others are underserved.

problems, self-esteem, and issues related to traumatic experiences. In addition to the regular meeting with their respective primary therapists, clients experience attention and help from a wider circle of caregivers. Moreover, during the course of treatment, individuals may attend different groups as they negotiate the goals and objectives of their individual care plans.

- An additional, or perhaps an alternative, approach is for the primary therapist of each client to provide therapeutic homework assignments. The written copy of the assignments is given to the childcare staff with specific instructions for follow-through. In this way, clients begin to see their place in the milieu as an expansion of their personal therapy. Aware of being more than a face in the crowd, they can see a program fit just for them. Is this a lot to deal with? Yes, which is a good argument for narrower fields of therapeutic work within an organization. But in dealing with the issues discussed, the devil lies in the logistics. If the groups are categorized by appropriate diagnoses and the homework is simple with proper follow-through, the stretching felt can be mitigated and kept to a minimum. Properly executed, the personalization of this approach can increase the clinical effectiveness of the program.

Summary

The examples provided in this chapter are only a small sampling of the multiplicity of issues that can arise when operating a treatment milieu. Weather analysts are well trained, look for special circumstances, and react with a warning if something inclement is on the horizon. Weather patterns are increasingly predictable when forecasters use all their tools. However, those of us who expect correct predictions of weather patterns know that sometimes the weatherman gets it all wrong. Even with advanced training and tools that help gauge what is coming, those in the behavioral health field should be prepared for the worst. In the spring we are wary of exploring a narrow canyon for fear that rain and flash floods will send us scrambling for higher ground. Consider a city in the West that has spent years and millions of dollars to retrofit famous buildings in the event of a catastrophic shaking. The same is true of weather issues on the East Coast, where walls are built to hold back the surging sea. It isn't a matter of *if*, it is a matter of *when*. There is plenty of precedence that gives us pause as we consider what to be prepared for venturing into our own mental health territories. In every scenario we consider the options and the procedural implementations before they face us head on. That keeps us safe and on track for success.

CHAPTER 5

Starve the Rogue

Dealing with the Negative "Power Broker"

JARED U. BALMER

O NE OF THE MOST DIFFICULT PROBLEMS MILIEU MANAGERS encounter is a single client who sucks the oxygen out of the milieu. The deviancy and noncompliance of such individuals demand the attention of group members and staff alike—all being negative. Mitigating such forces will test the very best communication skills of the caretakers.

The Problem: Joseph

Joe was admitted to a residential treatment facility. He had a history of chemical abuse and a brief brush with the law. His parents suffered through countless family arguments that always centered on Joe's insatiable need to push back on family rules and expectations. He refused any form of outpatient therapy. Joe was well past his seventeenth birthday. Deathly afraid of losing their son to drug addiction or other self-defeating behavior, they opted for residential care—much to Joe's dismay.

Joseph was tall and handsome. His bleached-blond hair was the topic of discussion among other clients at his treatment facility. Joseph was charming and well spoken. In the admitting interview with his therapist Joseph insisted he had no problems. "My family always over-reacts," he claimed. It did not take long for his two roommates to be in awe of young Joseph. His war stories of acquiring drugs and the experience of incredible trips, along with his ability to charm the ladies, were captivating. Joe did not speak with an overreaching vibrato. He was deliberate with a maturing tone. Suffice it to say, his two younger roommates were captured by him. To them, Joseph had street cred. It did not take long for this perception to spread to a large part of the client population. His "clever" challenging of the staff on the rules and regulation of the therapeutic community saw to that. Over the ensuing weeks, Joseph's charm and street cred had woven themselves into the fabric of the therapeutic milieu. His behavior, both overt and covert, had become one of the main topics with clients and staff alike.

The staff knew that they had a problem on their hands. Joe's mal-adaptive behavior had changed the flavor of the client community—the milieu. The healing influence of the prosocial milieu was greatly weakened by a single individual: the Power Broker, Joseph. Quick corrective action was required.

The Problem: Kate

When Kate turned fifteen, her parents knew that something was amiss. With increased frequency, she would call her parents to pick her up from school in the middle of the day, claiming that she had a migraine headache. Concerned by this trend, her parents took Kate to two medical doctors. Both of them insisted that they could not find anything physically that would support her claim. One of the physicians suggested that a psychiatric evaluation may shed further light on the problem. After a series of psychiatric evaluations, the picture emerged that Kate suffered from depression and low self-esteem. Consequently, Kate was referred to an outpatient clinic. However, after a few visits, she refused to go. When her parents put pressure on Kate to resume treatment, she became angry. Huge family fits ensued with increasing frequency, with Kate slamming doors and destroying various items in the house. After consultation with professionals, the parents admitted Kate to an outdoor behavioral health program.

No behavior outburst was noted in the wilderness program. What became evident was the fact that Kate kept the twelve-member client group hostage. Never angry or striking out at staff, she took two hours to get up in the morning. On hiking trips, she complained of an upset stomach, resulting in the cancellation of the activity. In the group discussion, Kate never spoke and answered questions from group members with "Yes," "No," or "I don't know." Nor did she collude with other peers to circumvent the rules and guidelines of the therapeutic community.

It was evident to the staff that Kate—although compliant in many ways—demanded the attention of the entire program. Much of the composite interaction of the therapeutic environment had to do with "What are we going to do with Kate? How can we help Kate?" or "We have to change our plans because of Kate." Something had to be done.

Instability Rules

Both of these examples are different on one level but share crucial behavior in common. Joe is actively attempting to spread his toxicity with a flashy, provocative, and challenging vibrato. Kate does none of these. She is quiet, and her behavior is a signal that she does not want to be involved. Assessing these clients individually, one has plenty of data to place them in different diagnostic categories. In fact, many professionals working with these two individuals would choose different treatment avenues. However, their effects on their communities of peers have much in common. Their behavior is such that they draw attention to themselves at the expense of other peers. Much of the interactions among peers and staff alike are focused on them. They become the dominating news story, leaving other peers in their wake. This leaves the caregivers with no other alternative but to grease the squeaky wheel. By displaying the most deviant behavior of the group, both Joe and Kate have become the Power Brokers of the therapeutic environment or milieu. They dictate the agenda. Their deviant behavior—deviant from the rest of the community—also is defined as the most unstable behavior of the group. It follows that instability rules.

> *Knowing how to intervene with the entire community or with the respective individuals is a skill that every childcare staff member must have. Without it, chaos takes over—chaos rules.*

Key variables like instability and social power, with their positive and negative implications for building and maintaining a prosocial therapeutic community, are best understood by examining the axioms of commination theory. Knowing how to intervene with the entire community or with the respective individuals is a skill that every childcare staff member must have. Without it, chaos takes over—chaos rules.

Axioms of Communication

1. THE IMPOSSIBILITY OF NOT COMMUNICATING

To say that a given person simply does not communicate is a complete misnomer. Likewise, expressing that a person with whom one intends to have a conversation simply is not communicating is utterly false. Behavior has no opposites. One cannot *not* behave. Humans' communication is defined by sending back-and-forth messages to each other—in essence, exchanging behavioral clues. Such messages may consist of words (the spoken language) but *always* include nonverbal language. Nonverbal messages include:

- Kinesics: Any and all body movement (facial expressions, eye movement, etc.)

- Voice quality: The inflection, cadence, and volume of speech

- Proxemics: The relative distance between people

- Olfactory quality: The smell of an individual (deodorant, perfume, sweetness, etc.)

- Clothing: The type of clothing one wears (or does not wear)

- Artifacts: Bracelets, necklaces, earrings, tattoos, etc.

The person who is asked to answer a question and only responds with silence is still communicating—sending a message—at the nonverbal level. Such nonverbal messages may, at times, be difficult to interpret. An individual may have to read into what the person is "saying" by the nonverbal behavior. Remember, one cannot *not* send messages. The young man in a group discussion looking straight ahead or the girl sitting at the dinner table with her eyes closed are likely comminuting that they do not want to communicate with others. In such a case, most people get the message and do not speak to them.

2. THE COMMAND ASPECT OF NONVERBAL COMMUNICATION

When two or more individuals communicate with each other, the nonverbal portion of each exchanged message clarifies (or obstructs) what is being said at the verbal level. The verbal part of the message conveys the content, and the nonverbal part of the message tells the recipient how to interpret the content. Therefore, the nonverbal part of the message is often referred to as the command aspect of the message. The smiling and touching behavior that accompanies the words "I like you" signals to the recipient how to interpret the words. Conversely, if "I like you" is accompanied by a frown and lack of eye contact, the interpretation of the message will be different.

3. DEFINING A RELATIONSHIP

As soon as two or more people meet, they begin immediately exchanging behaviors (verbal and nonverbal messages), attempting to define the nature of their relationship. This is to say that what is exchanged between individuals not only is information but also imposes behavior. The imposed behavior, the nonverbal exchange, is the ongoing way of defining the relationship of "This is how I see me ... this is how I see you ... this is how I see you seeing me." Such exchanges could potentially go on endlessly (Watzlawick et al. 1967). Exchanging messages with each other is more than exchanging information; it is always, under all circumstances, a way to *relate* to each other.

4. CONTROL IN A RELATIONSHIP

When Mike communicates a message (verbal or nonverbal) to Heidi, he is making a maneuver to define the relationship. In essence, Mike is telling Heidi, "This is the sort of relationship we have with each other."

It is now up to Heidi to accept or reject the attempt to define their relationship according to what Mike wants it to be. Heidi can counter Mike's "proposal" or send a message back, attempting to define the relationship to Heidi's liking. This interaction between two people is always characterized by two important issues—first, the types of messages or behavior that will take place in this relationship, and second, who will control what is to take place in the relationship and thereby define the relationship (Haley 1963). Because it is impossible not to communicate, the negotiations of defining the relationship are unavoidable. Consider the following: Mike is inviting Heidi to sit down, and Heidi responds by standing and remaining mute. Both parties are making an attempt to define the relationship to their liking—both want control in the relationship. On the other hand, if Heidi sits down, she has agreed to Mike's definition of the relationship, giving him control—at least for that moment. If Heidi turns around and walks away, she has rejected Mike's attempt to define the relationship and communicated a message to define the relationship according to her.

5. SYMMETRICAL, COMPLEMENTARY, METACOMPLEMENTARY, AND PARALLEL INTERACTION

All interactions between two individuals fall into one of four categories—that is to say that in any given moment in time, they interact in symmetrical, complementary, metacomplementary, or parallel exchanges (Bateson 1935).

Symmetrical interaction is defined by the exchange of the same behavior—loud for loud, weakness for weakness, good for good, friendly for friendly, etc. Picture two individuals yelling at each other or two people sitting across from each other, with neither saying a word, avoiding eye contact. A teacher scolds a student; the student responds by telling the teacher to get lost. Symmetrical interaction is characterized by each party's attempt to be in control—to define the relationship according to their ideation. This type of interaction will ultimately result in instability—an ongoing fight for power and control.

Complementary interaction is defined by the exchange of opposites—loud for quiet, strong for weak, good for bad, dominating for submissive, etc. Picture a group facilitator asking a group to pay attention, with the result of group members ceasing their chitchat and looking toward the leader. A teenager asks one of his peers to stop an annoying behavior, with that person complying with such a request. These interactions are typified with one person in control as the other individual accepts the nature of the relationship that is being suggested. In such a relationship, one person is in control. In other words, one person is in the "one-up" position, and the other person is in the "one-down" position. These relationships become static and ridged. A complementary interaction is dependent on one individual in control, with the other person agreeing to that arrangement.

Metacomplementary interaction is defined by a relationship in which the person in the one-down position is in control (Watzlawick 2011). How so? If Person A pretends to be helpless and is able to persuade Person B to behave in a certain way, Person A is in control of the relationship. Individuals who deliberately take the one-down position in order to achieve a particular outcome behave in a meta-complementary fashion. Consider this example: Max, a member of a scout troop, is charged with setting up the chairs for the upcoming troop meeting. He hates doing so. He tells Paul that he does not feel well and persuades him to do it. Max has successfully defined his relationship with Paul as metacomplementary. His helplessness put him in control.

Parallel interaction is the exchange of symmetrical, complementary, and metacomplementary interaction without the attempt to be in control. Depending on the circumstances, control in the relationship is freely given and taken. Individuals in a parallel relationship recognize that that is in their best interest to cooperate, providing each time for who has control at any given time.

Deviant Is King

In any group of two or more people, the individual that displays the most deviant behavior is the one in charge. Consider the following four scenarios:

1. A group of twelve individuals led by a group leader is sitting in a circle discussing a topic. A group member stands up, walks across the room, and stares out the window. Inevitably, the attention of all group members is focused on the individual at the window, wondering what is going on. The group leader asks the "window person" to return to his seat, but he does not comply.

2. Four individuals are asked by their supervisor to solve a problem. Not long after they begin their problem-solving task, one person begins to launch accusations and complaints about their boss. An argument about the boss's virtues and shortcomings ensues among the group.

3. An adolescent male begins to argue with the group leader, correcting her in a sarcastic fashion. The group leader profusely apologizes to the child for not having the facts straight and invites the youth to take over the group discussion.

4. A social study teacher lectures in front of a class of high school students. They all listen intently. Intermittently, some students raise their hands to ask questions. The teacher answers the question and continues with the lecture.

With the exception of scenario #4, control of power in the interaction between group members is at stake. The individual who has the control and power in these examples is most easily recognized by the one who displays the most deviant behavior from the normative group behavior. It is important to recognize that the term *deviant* does not refer to bad behavior but simply to different-from-normal behavior of any group at any given time.

In example #1, the window person is behaving in a deviant or different fashion from the rest of the group. The collective attention from all others moves in that individual's direction, giving that person power and control. Moreover, the window person is attempting to define his relationship as complementary with the rest of the group. Complementary interaction is always a power grab. The same attempt is made by the complainer in example #2. However, the other members are drawn into a symmetrical relationship, all fighting for power and control. The original group task has been sacrificed on the altar of who can be the most persuasive. In example #3, the group leader did not take the bait. She purposely took the metacomplementary position, implying that the youth knew better. What is critical to understand in this circumstance is that she gave the youth permission to be the leader. Any person giving permission to another person is, by definition of communication theory, in charge or in control. Why? Because the person who has been granted permission is in compliance with the one who gave the permission. In essence, that person is following the orders of the one giving permission. Those who grant permission are always in the one-up position, retaining control in the relationship. The struggles for control and power are absent in example #4. In a parallel interaction, each party takes their turn with being heard.

Starve the Rogue

Caregivers who are charged with leading a therapeutic group aimed at changing behavior will often be plagued by participants who attempt to divert the process. Such a rogue member or Power Broker can have a devastating influence on the entire milieu. They suck the oxygen away from others, demanding an inordinate amount of attention and provide significant challenges for those charged with creating and maintaining a healthy milieu. When needed, having interventions and strategies readily available can make the difference between a healthy or unhealthy environment. Below are examples of such interventions.

DEALING WITH RESISTANCE

We have established the fact that the most deviant member of a group is in control. Their communication, verbally or nonverbally, is a move to define the relationship with the rest of the group as complementary. They are in a power position dictating the flow and direction of the group interaction. Whether an individual does this consciously or unconsciously is irrelevant. Their deviant behavior—deviant from the collective behavior of the group—automatically places them in the power position. In a group aimed at changing from maladaptive to prosocial behavior, the Power Broker signals to the rest of its members that he or she is resisting such an attempt. Such an individual has hijacked the control away from the group leader. Getting control back becomes the main objective of the group leader.

Consider the following example. A group member says to the group leader, "I don't know what you want from me. You go ahead to tell me every step of the way what I should do." On the surface it appears that the group member has empowered, or given control to, the group leader. However, the opposite is true. The group member has directed the group leader on what to do. He is defining the relationship as complementary. He is giving orders. He is in control (Haley 1963). This apparent paradox is seated in the notion of *who* is giving orders to *whom*. In this example, the group member is essentially communicating to the group leader, "Obey my command to tell me what to do."

Example 1

A group member gets out of his chair, stands up, and screams, "This is ridiculous!" The group member has displayed the most deviant behavior of the group. He is in control. The collective attention from the rest of the group is directed to that individual. Understating that the most deviant group member is in control, the group leader fundamentally has two choices in responding to the oppositional member. He can raise the ante and display even more deviant behavior (e.g., screaming louder, getting into the faces of the group members, etc.). Such interventions will lead to a symmetrical relationship with both parties attempting to be in control—with no winner. A far more effective way to intervene is to grant permission to the group member to be disagreeable, essentially telling him what to do.

Group Member: "I do not agree with what you are proposing. This is ridiculous."

Group Leader: "For whatever reason, which I cannot determine, you have a strong need to disagree with what we are discussing. There is nothing I can do to control your outburst. You are totally in control of your own behavior. Let us know when you can rejoin our discussion."

Rather than falling into the trap of a symmetrical relationship or completely surrendering to the demands of the individual, the group leader regains control by defining the relationship as metacomplementary. This is achieved on two levels: first, by implicitly granting permission to continue with his deviant behavior, and second, by admitting helplessness over the negative interruption of the group discussion. In reality, the team leader is prescribing the very maladaptive symptoms the group member is displaying. The hope of this intervention rests on the assumption that the deviant group member does not want to follow the order of the group leader. The only way he can do so is by resisting the implicit order of the leader and behave in a different way. Of course, there is no absolute guarantee that the individual will do so. However, the likelihood for the deviant group member to cease and desist with the inappropriate behavior is far better than entering the shouting match. Mental health clinicians know such techniques as symptom prescription. It works on the basis that the deviant individual implicitly knows that his or her behavior is not normative but inappropriate under the circumstances.

Many individuals entering therapy resist change. This is particularly the case for adolescents who demonstrate oppositional behaviors. Unfortunately, some helping professionals cannot resist giving endless advice to those individuals by engaging in the "Why don't you—yes, but" game (Berne 1964). Such a symmetrical relationship is fruitless, as both parties attempt to stay in control without any therapeutic gain. This game can stop instantly if the therapist steps out of the advisor role by asking the question, "Why should you change?" This changes the relationship to metacomplementary by implicitly confessing helplessness while, at the same time, directing the client toward self-reflection. By doing so, resistance is turned into a vehicle of change.

Example 2

Alexa, a fourteen-year-old girl, refused to get up at the designated time. She was newly admitted to a boarding school, and the daily schedule called for breakfast to be served at 8:00 a.m. This cat-and-mouse game had been going on for over a week, as staff members attempted to bribe, encourage, and sternly lecture her in hopes of compliance. Alexa was examined by the school nurse, and no physical maladies were identified that would prevent her from getting up on time. Alexa, however, was determined that no one was going to tell her when to get up.

Dorm counselor: "Alexa, by now, it is obvious that you have no intention to get up on time. We read you loud and clear. We, as a staff, have discussed your situation and determined that you can stay in bed as long as you want. Some two years ago, we had a young student who also refused to get up. His record was thirty-nine days. So when the students leave campus for various recreational activities, we'll leave a couple of dorm counselors behind to check on you to be sure you are safe."

> The worst punishment for virtually all adolescents is social isolation—the inability to interact with their peers.

Intimating or psychically forcing Alexa out of bed is a disastrous, no-win situation. Since she is not causing any harm to people and property, the "no-intervention" intervention will likely produce the best results. As long as Alexa refuses to get up, she remains in control. She is in the power position, as getting up is an implied rule. Giving her permission to stay in bed is the same as "telling" her to say in bed. Moreover, telling her that the record for staying in bed is thirty-nine days will discourage her from lasting that long. Missing recreational activities becomes an additional incentive to abandon the "I will not get up" routine. The only way Alexa can resist being told what to do is getting up on time. Furthermore, the worst punishment for virtually all adolescents is social isolation—the inability to interact with their peers.

Example 3

Keven turned nineteen years of age when he entered a young adult transition program designed to cement life skills in preparation for independent living. The mixed-gender group of peers met daily for a problem-solving group. For a week, Keven took a high profile within the group interaction. His frequent comments did not rise to the level of viciousness or personal attacks but had a certain quality of bad humor. His peers grew increasingly tired of Keven's behavior, and the group leader spent much of the session redirecting Keven to participate in a more mature fashion. Holding true to the fact that the most deviant member of a group is in charge, Keven controlled the group. Appropriate group behavior comprised much of the one-on-one interaction between Keven and the group leader. Miraculously, Keven's group behavior was void of his long string of bad humor. At the end of that group, the group leader made the following comments.

Group Leader: "Keven, we all noticed that you avoided making your usual comments that distracted from the objectives of the group discussion. I want to caution you to go slow. I know that you have figured out that participating in the group process in a more appropriate way gets you the support of your peers. It is remarkable what you have done. However, being realistic, a sharp turnaround, miraculous as it is, is often followed by a relapse. So please go slow in your progression toward a more prosocial style of peer interaction. I think you should have a few relapses."

Mental health professionals know that virtually all miraculous changes do not last. Recognizing this truth, the group leader prescribes a relapse into old behaviors. By doing so, he is telling Keven what to do and regaining control in the relationship. Moreover, the group leader is bringing Keven's inappropriate behavior to the attention of the group, implicitly challenging him in front of his peers to behave appropriately but giving him permission to continue. The only way for Keven to resist is to change his behavior.

Example 4

Susan had a long history of involvement with psychotherapy. After two years of outpatient therapy with virtually no progress, her parents opted to send her to an outdoor behavior health program. After a few weeks, she managed to run away and was subsequently placed in a secure residential treatment center. After eighteen months at the RTC, the childcare staff, in concert with the parents, thought it best to send Susan to a therapeutic boarding school. The reason was that Susan still showed a measurable amount of opposition and resistance to change. In sum, Susan had been involved in therapy for over four years. The clinical staff at the therapeutic boarding school was smart enough to figure out that Susan was not about to turn over a completely new leaf and wholeheartedly embrace compliance and healthy behavior. Specifically, the clinical director recognized that expressing confidence and optimism in helping Susan to change would simply pay into her hands in "conquering" yet one more therapist. A rookie therapist would have been trapped into asking Susan, "How can I help you?" Not so this clinical director:

Clinical director: "Susan, can you provide me with a history of your involvements with psychotherapy?"

Susan: "I saw a therapist in my hometown."

Clinical director: "How long did you see him, and what did you get out of him?"

Susan: "I saw him for two years, and really, it was a waste of time."

Clinical director: "Where did you go next?"

Susan: "My parents sent me off to a wilderness program."

Clinical director: "Tell me about that."

(Susan goes on to explain in detail the experience at the wilderness program.)

Clinical director (goes into great and lengthy detail to inquire of Susan all the interventions that were attempting to help her change for the last four years—unsuccessfully so. He understands that having Susan provide him with a complete, expansive history of failure all along the way is helping him for the following intervention): "Susan, I have been a therapist for a long time. I have dealt with adolescents over and over again. But never have I come across a case as hopeless as yours. After listening to your story of what seemed to be an endless immersion into therapy, I can tell you with much authority that you put way too much credence into therapy. Endless hours of therapy can never help you to get where you want to go. Maybe what we can help you with is how to learn to live with these issues that have plagued you for so long."

For many years, Susan has been in the power position in all of her relationships with individuals attempting to help her change. Regardless of the underlying reason for her protractive behavior, she defined the relationships with all her helpers as complementary—one-up. Here, the clinician changes the rules of interaction completely by claiming that therapy will not work. The only way that Susan can resist is by proving that there may be a chance that therapy might just be helpful.

Example 5

At fifteen years of age, Max was exceptionally tall for his age. He had gotten into some trouble during his freshman year in high school by teasing and intermittently intimidating his peers. He was not particularly a great student. He only had one or two friends, whom his parents disapproved of. He tried out to make the junior varsity basketball team but did not make the cut. His parents were convinced that it had something to do with his marginal peer relationships. Following this setback, Max's behavior deteriorated. He became increasingly oppositional. When he refused to participate in individual and family therapy and skipped school on a regular basis, the parents opted to send Max to a residential treatment center.

During the first few weeks at the treatment center, Max was flying under the radar. Checking out his new surroundings, he was taking note of the parameters of what was permissible and forbidden behavior. However, soon after this honeymoon period, Max tried out his maladaptive behaviors on peers and staff alike. Ignoring directions from staff, treating peers with disrespect, and pouting when given feedback by staff and peers became increasingly more frequent. Max demanded a lot of attention, as his negative influence became a force to be reckoned with. Telling, begging, and encouraging Max to change produced little or no results. A change in approach was called for.

Therapist: "Max, have you ever heard about the developmental stages of development?"

Max: "Do you mean like growing up?"

Therapist: "Yes. We know there are five stages of human development. First is infancy, where the baby is completely dependent on others and incapable of delaying gratification, like food. Second, childhood, where the child is learning to interact with others, share his toys, and get along with others. Does any of this make sense?"

Max: "Yeah, I guess."

Therapist: "The next stage is called adolescence. Most people call it the teenage years. This is a period where many changes take place. Hormones make you grow hair in places where you never had any. Your voice changes. You develop a psychosexual sense of yourself. You become more mature. You learn abstract reasoning, become more empathetic to others—in short, you are growing to be an adult. I'm sure you've heard about this before."

Max: "Of course."

Therapist: "Now, Max, the entire staff here has been talking much about your behavior. It's obvious that some of your behavior is reminiscent of preadolescent behavior."

Max: "What are you talking about?"

Therapist: "Many of your behaviors, like being insensitive to others, dominating discussions, intermittently being oppositional, et cetera, is indicative that your maturity level, when it comes to interaction with peers and adults, is lagging behind your physical maturity level. The fact that you did not respond favorably when encouraged to quit these behaviors is proving the fact that you show a delay of what we typically see from an age-appropriate adolescent. We know that working through these developmental stages is important. In fact, not having worked through these stages appropriately has negative implications for the next stage. So the quickest way to make it to the next maturational stage is to get these undesirable behaviors out of your system. So we encourage you to increase these behaviors and get them out of your system so that you can successfully enter into the next maturational stage. I will tell your peers what you are working on so that they are not surprised when you engage in these behaviors. Remember, the more you do this, the quicker you can move on."

Max has not responded to traditional "Please stop" interventions. By continuing with his negative behavior, Max is in control. This unconventional intervention has a much better chance to succeed based on the following elements:

- Max's maladaptive behavior is reframed as normative, albeit assigned to a lower stage of maturity.

- The therapist gives Max permission to continue with his negative behavior. By doing so, he implicitly admits helplessness and defines the relationship as metacomplementary, with the therapist (in fact, the entire staff) in the one-up position.

- Max is placed in a bind. By continuing with his maladaptive behavior, he agrees that he is immature. Much of his behavior is Max's misguided attempt to be mature, dominant, and in charge of defining the nature of his relationships. To prove that he is mature is to abandon the maladaptive behavior.

Feed the Leader

Rightfully so, we described with some detail how to deal with rogue individuals directly. Conversely, there are avenues of how to attempt to keep the rogue group member in check through indirect intervention. This is primarily accomplished by elevating and recognizing those individuals who are invested in making a positive contribution to themselves or to the environment as a whole. Formally recognizing the most improved behavior of a group member, attending a concert, participating in an adventure activity, or going to a movie are just a few examples of an endless list of activities afforded those who are not overtly or covertly resisting change. By comparison, the rogue individual is excluded from these activities. "Feeding the leader" thus becomes an activity to balance the scale of attention. This is particularly important for those group members who often get the short end of the stick, as the rogue individual attempts to dominate the therapeutic environment by his or her deviancy.

Summary

Power Brokers can often derail the goals and objectives of any purposeful group by displaying the most deviant behavior within the community. Their deviant behavior demands attention, leaving the group leadership with the challenge of returning the group discussion to its original intention. In virtually all cases, Power Brokers resist personal change or attempt to disrupt the therapeutic milieu to aid their maladaptive intention. Verbal confrontation of such negative behavior is often fruitless when the Power Broker persists with the unwanted behavior—proving that he has control. For staff members to regain control of the group or milieu, defining the relationship with the Power Broker as metacomplementary stands an infinitely better chance than ongoing confrontation, encouragement, or threats of consequences. Short of causing harm to individuals or doing major destruction to property, symptom prescription holds a much better chance to return to normality. Giving the Power Broker permission to continue with the maladaptive behavior places him or her in a bind in which further resistance becomes compliant behavior and changes the entire meaning of the relationship.

References

Bateson, G. "Culture, Contact, and Schismogenesis." *Manuscript 35* (1935): 178–83.

Berne, Eric. *Games People Play*. New York: Simon & Schuster, 1964.

Haley, J. *Strategies of Psychotherapy*. New York: Grune & Stratton, Inc., 1963.

Watzlawick, P., J. Beavin-Bavelas, and D. D. Jackson. *Pragmatic of Human Communication; A Study of Interactional Patters, Pathologies, and Paradoxes*. New York: W. W. Norton & Company, 1967.

Watzlawick, P., J. H. Weakland, and R. Fisch. *Change: Principles of Problem Formation and Problem Resolution*. New York: W. W. Norton & Company, 2011.

CHAPTER 6

Managing the Underground

Learning Lessons from Distractive Forces

R. MICHAEL BULLOCH

T AKE A MOMENT TO CONSIDER THE UNIQUE SETTING OF A
therapeutic community, where a group of people from
diverse backgrounds share time and space for an extended
period during incredibly difficult times in their lives. The cast of characters must coexist, regardless
of different personalities, ages,
strengths and deficits, levels of
skill development, maturity, life
experiences, insight, and willingness to address issues. Not only
do these factors occur independently, collectively, and simultaneously, but residents also are
geographically separated from

> The goal of the milieu
> is to reinforce and
> promote a therapeutic
> framework that
> provides safety, models
> mutual respect, and
> encourages growth.

their families and friends and are flooded with uncertainty for their immediate and long-term futures. No small feat!

The goal of the milieu is to reinforce and promote a therapeutic framework that provides safety, models mutual respect, and encourages growth. Certain difficulties and dynamics can (and will) take place in therapeutic communities, which require staff to respond in highly individualized and strategic manners. One of the most important steps in creating and maintaining a healthy environment is to take proactive steps that reduce the frequency and volatility of difficulties that can occur: "An ounce of prevention is worth a pound of cure." In other words, be proactive. It is less difficult (and more prudent) to initiate steps that prevent problems than it is to address and repair damage to the community after problems occur.

With this in mind, there are a number of foundational characteristics that should be present in therapeutic communities. The environment must reflect emotional and physical safety, and staff must model respect toward students and colleagues. All staff should understand program policies and expectations and demonstrate consistency. Residents must understand the rationale (the "why") behind what they are being asked to do and *how* their participation directly benefits them and the community. Policy and procedures must promote safety, respect, order, and cleanliness. Staff should be positive and engaged and *respond* to problems versus *react* to issues that arise.

Choose Your Own Adventure

Case vignettes provide staff with opportunities to conceptualize problematic situations, utilize critical thinking skills, look for clues that might provide useful information that may otherwise be missed, and formulate responses ... kind of like a "choose your own adventure" for those working in mental health fields. Case vignettes that are often most helpful are those that pivot in different directions than anticipated or present an approach one disagrees with. Vignettes provide opportunities to compare and contrast potential solutions to everyday events in therapeutic environments.

The following case studies represent common episodes and interactions that occur in treatment settings. The purpose of a therapeutic setting is not about creating a sterile environment where nothing can go wrong or where residents obediently and consistently make the best choices that positively reflect the merits of the program. The therapeutic milieu should aspire to be an environment where residents and staff alike are given opportunities to make mistakes and learn from them. Vignettes are useful for those new to the field and can provide examples to brainstorm interventions with colleagues. Despite the variety of examples offered in this chapter, few interventions result in immediate, observable change, and no single method works all the time.

The Problem: "Can You Keep a Secret?"

A therapeutic boarding school allows access to technology after adolescents demonstrate specific skills, such as time management and prioritization. Students must adhere to strict parameters regarding computer use. Expectations include refraining from visiting inappropriate sites, making negative comments about students and staff, or revealing personal information that may compromise a student's confidentiality. Despite these boundaries, certain residents ignore the contracts they have signed.

A student has returned from a home visit. He secretly brings unauthorized external software that bypasses facility firewalls, cloaks user activities, and allows for unfettered internet access. Within weeks, the bypass program is shared among residents. During supervised computer time, a group of residents manages to create a clandestine Reddit subreddit forum that can only be accessed via an invite into the group. Within the exclusive forum, students make homophobic, misogynistic, and disparaging comments directed at students and staff.

Despite the online forum being secret, additional students become aware of the group's existence and about the software hack that enables access. No one wants to bring it up to staff, because the residents behind the hack are intelligent, funny, and popular. Thus, the instigators have a significant influence on the community. If others reveal their methods, there is a high likelihood that whistleblowers will become new targets for retaliation. The forum continues for a month until a couple of students finally come forward. These residents feel guilty for being passively involved and not saying anything earlier. They do not want to be identified for coming forward, or others will call them narcs. These residents show staff the comments made in the forum. Since usernames do not reflect actual names, it is difficult to identify all who are involved and those who are behind various statements made. Many comments are particularly offensive, and while some are directed at students, staff are the primary targets. Incidentally, a staff member mentioned in numerous negative comments is going through difficult personal matters. This situation requires a careful approach that supports those who have come forward and those who've been targeted. Moreover, the approach must provide opportunities for instigators to identify their thoughts, feelings, and experiences that have contributed to repetitive, secretive, and disparaging actions toward others.

CONSIDERATIONS FOR SOLUTIONS

Like the human body, therapeutic communities express symptoms that can reveal a healthy environment or an ailing system. Some symptoms reveal the normal wear and tear of daily life in communal settings, such as arguing, blaming, and exhibiting negative attention-seeking behaviors. The presence of these symptoms may not indicate major community issues. Episodes of arguing, blaming, and struggling to compromise will occur and should be expected. Yet there are times when symptoms can reveal the subtle or not-so-subtle presence of significant issues lurking below the surface. Like the proverbial iceberg, what is unobservable may cause significant harm. Among all potential signs and symptoms of an unhealthy community, *secrets* are the most severe symptoms that can lead to titanic breakdowns.

> Among all potential signs and symptoms of an unhealthy community, secrets are the most severe symptoms that can lead to titanic breakdowns.

The majority of community members may not be actively involved in sharing secrets. However, they may know what's going on behind the scenes, even though they don't reveal their knowledge. Examples may include a few members of the community actively planning or engaging in unhealthy decisions, such as an AWOL attempt, bringing back contraband from a home visit, or stealing from another resident. Group members often comment that since a situation does not directly involve them, they choose not to get involved out of fear of social repercussions. Being told a secret may make one feel like a member of an exclusive club—especially for an adolescent. Individuals who are keeping the secret possess something of social value and may feel special as a result. As time goes on, these feelings may morph into "If I tell on them, they will tell on me." The ripple effect of secret agreements reveals a lack of transparency and trust within the group, fears of being vulnerable, and a pervasive sense of mounting discomfort. A primary deterrent from sharing secrets with staff members stems from the questions "Have I done something wrong?" and "What will happen next?"

In the problem described above, there are many dynamics taking place in the community that pose unique ramifications for students and staff. However, the immediate issue is a lack of emotional safety within the greater community. Many students in therapeutic settings have experienced mistreatment through bullying and cyberbullying. Always remember that current events in the milieu can trigger past traumatic experiences. When negative events like these occur, students will attempt to appraise their surroundings for potential threats. The primary question from residents is inevitably, "Am I safe?"

Community members need to feel safe and must feel that others will be held accountable for their actions, no matter how much social power certain individuals possess. It is intimidating to be the target of any attacks. Moreover, it's intimidating for those who are not initial targets but wonder what may happen if they lose favor with certain residents. The uncertainty surrounding these questions creates tremendous anxiety, division, and fear. As a result, the primary response goal is to restore a sense of safety within the community. Safety is measured by how staff and the community respond to problems that arise. When residents observe immediate and proportionate responses to safety issues, they feel secure, understood, and validated.

Students need to know that staff will address matters with urgency, will ask the right questions, and will respond fairly. Challenging moments like these provide real opportunities for students to develop social skills, advocate for themselves, set healthy boundaries with peers, face uncertainty, and increase distress tolerance. When shared secrets are purposely kept from staff, they compromise community safety, build division, and contribute to an *us* (residents) versus *them* (staff) culture. If students feel that "staff can't find out," the message promotes the narrative that staff members are opponents. Therefore, responses to students must be fair minded and proportionate, so staff members do not feed or perpetuate this narrative.

The appropriate response for this scenario requires a greater community approach. Staff members representing each department should participate in ensuing group meetings to process and demonstrate a school-wide response. Since the issue affects all constituents (and is more than merely a milieu issue), the response requires an all-hands-on-deck approach. Doing so sends a verbal and nonverbal message to the community, reinforces school support, promotes safety, and validates those who've been hurt by derogatory comments.

Another goal of community meetings is to help the instigators (who have maneuvered themselves into a corner) to work their way out. Despite the outward bravado and indifference guilty residents may exhibit, they are often extremely critical and disappointed in themselves when their behaviors become known. During these groups, staff must be aware of their own life experiences and emotions (particularly the difficult ones) and must understand their triggers. Conversely, staff must avoid perpetuating division by making the issue about themselves versus the student(s) in question. They must operate from a purpose that maintains safety and provides supportive opportunities for all group members to assert themselves and develop skills, such as self-reflection, acceptance of personal responsibility, conflict resolution, problem solving, and the process of making amends with those they have harmed.

When calling a group meeting, let students know that information has been brought to light that involves cyberbullying within the community. Provide responsible parties an opportunity to take ownership. Unfortunately, those directly involved don't always take immediate accountability. Some will only do so when they've exhausted all other alternatives or when their statements have been proven false. It's very likely that some members of the community are fearful of addressing the issue in group sessions, because they may have experienced online bullying in the past and worry about ramifications. As group meetings unfold, additional secrets may come out once the dam breaks. Be prepared to address potential fallout.

Milieu staff must be careful when addressing students who are involved. A common tactic among instigators is to find a way to become the victim, as opposed to the aggressor (e.g., "Staff is so unfair to me" or "The group shamed me"). Another challenge for staff is determining how much group time should be spent addressing the problem, particularly when the instigators and participants are not forthcoming about their involvement. Sometimes well-intentioned groups take far longer than they should, with the discussion moving in circles. Moreover, marathon groups can impact the schedule in negative ways, particularly for academic class time. As time goes on, other students (who had little to no involvement) grow frustrated because some of their peers are not being candid, their stories continue to change, or their own time is being wasted.

Staff must communicate with colleagues as to why the group is being called and convey the goals of the group intervention, so key department members can attend. If staff members are targeted by derogatory comments (particularly new staff or those who may be experiencing life challenges of their own), spend extra time processing the situation with them. Validate them, and reinforce a position of support. Regardless of whether the comments were made by a student undergoing mental health treatment, negative comments can still hurt and lead to resentments and burnout. Consider giving staff who are negatively impacted time off, and assess future interactions they may have with the offending students.

Finally, schedule a meeting with the staff member(s) who were assigned to monitor students during computer time, as they may overly rely on system firewalls, leading to decreased vigilance. The time it takes to create a subreddit forum, add user accounts, and write numerous comments about multiple staff and students appears to have occurred over time—as opposed to being an isolated incident. Questions about how staff members monitor clients during computer time must be addressed directly, and heightened policies and procedures should be implemented to prevent similar problems.

Summary

- Determine whether any posted information violates the confidentiality of students in the community (i.e., user names or pictures).

- Identify students with histories of trauma who can be triggered by this event.

- Be aware that staff members can be triggered by events based on their own experiences and histories.

- Demonstrate a sense of urgency and importance in addressing the issue within the group. Include staff from all departments to participate in groups in order to reinforce the message that this is a school-wide issue of great significance.

- Reinforce the importance of emotional and physical safety within the community.

- Respect the anonymity of those who shared their concerns with staff.

- Identify potential opportunities that exist, such as developing skills, confronting past trauma through self-advocacy, setting boundaries with others, and developing increased distress tolerance.

- Reinforce that staff must not make this about them by how they respond.

- Communicate with staff from different departments about the goals of the group meeting, why additional time is required, and how it may impact other elements of programming. Find ways to minimize the impact on class/academic schedules.

- Validate students and staff who are targeted by the negative remarks.

- Help those who have backed themselves into a corner to find a way out. Remember that despite outward appearances, there are likely internal conflicts for those who were involved. These moments offer opportunities to teach and develop empathy and awareness.

- Evaluate the appropriateness of offending students remaining in the program if they continue to engage in behaviors that target individuals and compromise the safety of the community, as they may require greater levels of care.

- Communicate and document details, so all staff and faculty have timely and accurate information.

- Look for lessons and learn from mistakes.

The Problem: "Liar, Liar!"

A group of adolescent residents is upset and feels staff members have lied to them about a planned activity that has been rescheduled. On the day of the initial event, a few staff call in sick, and a student in the community has been placed on safety precautions (requiring one-to-one staff supervision and impacting staffing ratios). Despite the unexpected circumstances, residents are frustrated and tell peers that staff cannot be trusted and don't honor their commitments. Ironically, some of the same students routinely omit or alter information, particularly when it helps them avoid accountability. It is winter, and the weather is wet and cold, with declining daylight hours. As a result, members of the community feel cooped up and bored. Soon residents promote the narrative that staff members are liars who can't be trusted. Other clients support the narrative out of boredom and distraction. While some students may not outwardly participate in the disruption, they whisper and pass notes behind the scenes. With little warning, a pervasive feeling of mistrust is on the brink.

CONSIDERATIONS FOR SOLUTIONS

Outside activities provide opportunities for students to have fun and relax while recharging their batteries for the important work they are facing. Sometimes staff members fail to recognize just *how* important activities are to residents. Regardless of whether there are legitimate reasons for rescheduling a planned activity, it's necessary to validate the students and let them vent. Staff must be willing to listen to their feelings, or they won't listen to staff. Milieu staff should respond rather than react and provide a thorough explanation of what has occurred that resulted in the schedule change. Give students a chance to express themselves. Though it can be tricky to determine how much time to allow them to vent, their voices matter beyond the present incident. If staff members don't allow enough time to process student grievances, residents may not feel their opinions or feelings count. However, providing too much time can unintentionally stoke fires that burn rapidly out of control, resulting in the community feeling discouraged, marginalized, and resentful.

While certain members of the community may express anger or use the situation to create drama or division, now is not the time to address it in a group setting. Consider speaking one on one with individual students, and pass the information on to the treatment team. Now is the time to validate and determine therapeutic opportunities (lessons). As staff members demonstrate a desire to listen, students are simultaneously given the opportunity to address frustrations and disappointment. The situation offers both staff and students moments to practice communication, proportionate responses, and problem-solving skills. When staff exhibit openness and understanding, students can transition from negative thoughts and experiences back to daily activities and move forward.

> Give them a voice in identifying possible alternatives, and give them options. Doing so provides opportunities to develop practical skills in the context of a situation that really matters to them.

Once staff members have provided residents with opportunities to express their frustrations (and student responses become repetitive), move on to the next step in the process, which is problem solving. If there are students who need more time to vent, consider using art therapy to express what needs to be said. Give them a voice in identifying possible alternatives, and give them options. Doing so provides opportunities to develop practical skills in the context of a situation that really matters to them.

With the poor weather, shorter days, and increased seasonal illness from staff and students, these situations are more likely to occur. Now is the time to enhance recreational programming, so activities are creative and balanced. Develop backup plans. Doing so will increase student morale and establish student relationships that are based on positive shared experiences rather than complaints and frustrations. When practical, make it a point to give community members time to make recommendations and consider various options and alternatives.

Summary

- Provide an explanation of why the activity needs to be rescheduled; be careful not to be rigid or defensive.

- Give students time to vent and express their feelings.

- Provide opportunities to demonstrate and teach flexibility, effective communication, and problem-solving skills.

- Validate.

- Move the discussion toward alternatives and problem solving when negative comments are repeated.

- Recognize and reinforce students who demonstrate proportionate responses to the situation or who model flexibility while transitioning from venting to problem solving.

- Provide students options and choices, and include them in the process.

- Create backup plans that staff can easily initiate when activities must be rescheduled due to weather, staffing ratios, or the need for social distancing.

- Communicate and document details, so all staff and faculty have timely and accurate information.

- Look for lessons, and learn from mistakes.

The Problem: "No Clue"

Jeff and Ben are in residential treatment due to ongoing difficulties with impulsivity, substance dependency, self-harm, depression, and anxiety. They routinely state that they have no clue why they are in treatment. Each has spent considerable time in previous treatment settings that include intensive outpatient and day-treatment therapy, multiple inpatient hospitalizations for self-harm, and wilderness therapy. Jeff and Ben both externalize reasons for their frustrations and discontent, blaming their feelings on the current program and community. They say they don't need help, that treatment is pointless, and the program is out to take their parents' money. Ben and Jeff minimize their issues and those of their peers. They say, "Your parents overreacted just like mine. You shouldn't be here either." Each misunderstands the intentions of others who offer support or from peers who are open to talking about their challenges and take active steps to address them. Ben and Jeff call these residents "a bunch of ass kissers."

Others in the community take notice of the dynamic duo and don't want to be targeted with insults and labels. Students are cautious of how they engage with Ben or Jeff. Over time, the two gain considerable influence within the milieu. During group meetings, residents quickly look to Ben and Jeff to gauge their approval and overall moods before participating. It becomes evident that other students are more concerned with how Ben and Jeff perceive them than they are about expressing their true thoughts and emotions. As the two residents continue these behaviors, their peers pay very close attention to how staff will respond, as they feel ambivalent about working on their treatment plans publicly. This pattern can shift community dynamics, limit communication, and decrease individual and collective progress. Over time, the pattern can create a disingenuous atmosphere that takes careful response and action to reverse.

CONSIDERATIONS FOR SOLUTIONS

Much of the problem can be explained by the fact that Ben's and Jeff's goals do not align with their parents' goals or the treatment team's focus. If either student had a physical ailment (such as a broken arm), there would be little disagreement about the treatment approach. The plan would likely include using an x-ray to assess the damage, alleviating immediate pain, and setting the bone so it will heal properly. Mental health issues aren't always evident or obvious, but if left unaddressed, they pose greater risks than broken bones. One of the primary challenges mental health professionals face is the common disconnect between the goals of struggling adolescent clients and the goals and objectives of their parents and the attending treatment teams.

If there remains ongoing disagreement, there is a greater likelihood of volitional treatment-interfering behaviors (TIBs) that may occur with students and parents. Treatment-interfering behaviors include refusing to acknowledge or discuss one's negative contributions or difficulties, being unwilling to work on therapy assignments, and possessing tools that could improve immediate situations but choosing not to use them. The lack of shared goals, combined with treatment-interfering behaviors, presents the single greatest barrier to client progress. Treatment-interfering behaviors originate from many factors. In this situation TIBs occur because there is a lack of shared goals, compounded by Ben's and Jeff's treatment fatigue and their ambivalence about making changes that are required to truly address issues.

Staff should not view Ben and Jeff as problems in the community, but as young people who have spent considerable time in numerous treatment settings and have given up hope that they can get out of the system and return to live with friends and family. Students like Ben and Jeff have been in treatment for so long that they feel like they are each rowing a boat where they can no longer see the shore from whence they left or any land in sight. Ultimately, Jeff and Ben feel as though they are drifting and making no progress at all. To put it simply, they are tired of rowing.

At one point in the process, Ben and Jeff may have had hope and may have put forth more effort. Now each needs tangible goals that reveal forward movement and progress. Rather than getting stuck on differences regarding goals, it's time to search for common ground. Identify areas (regardless of significance) where there is consensus toward shared goals. When common goals are identified, build upon them, and develop rewards that appeal to Ben and Jeff. By reinforcing their improvements, other students will understand that Jeff and Ben are not surrendering to staff or to the will of their parents, but they are adapting to situations that provide them with skills, direction, relief, and hope.

Discuss the differences between surrendering and adapting. Reinforce the message that Jeff and Ben are making decisions that benefit themselves and are taking control of the direction they want their lives to move toward. Sometimes staff can fall into patterns where they focus on what students aren't doing well rather than on what they are doing well. This perception can prevent staff from noticing when a student is trending in a positive direction, as progress can also be measured by a reduction of negative behaviors and routines, rather than solely upon the presence of positive forward movement. If staff only focus on positive steps as signs of progress, they may fail to recognize improvements that occur through incremental, decreased negative behaviors and routines. Staff should "catch" problematic students doing positive things in the community, such as helping a peer or demonstrating a willingness to compromise. It's important that well-intentioned staff be aware of their own potential rigidity that can perpetuate power struggles as they search for opportunities to validate client discouragement and treatment fatigue. Staff must help Ben and Jeff understand that by adapting their perceptions and behaviors, they will move further away from the negative interactions they don't want—toward the positive life experiences they seek.

Consider the rewards for Ben and Jeff that are associated with the premise: "I don't know why I'm here" and what variables may contribute to a lack of motivation to address treatment goals. Both boys complain to staff about program structure, other students, being away from home, wrongly placed in treatment, etc. Yet they are unwilling to participate in their own treatment process. This rigid perspective and stance offer evidence of why the boys cycle through various treatment programs. However, the cycle can be stopped.

Summary

- Validate treatment fatigue.

- Find mutual goals students possess that align with their parents' goals and the treatment plan.

- Create rewards that are important to students.

- Reinforce the importance of adaptation, and frequently review the differences between surrendering to the wills of others versus adapting to the environment. Reinforce that students control their progress.

- Catch students being engaged and doing something positive.

- Help students develop relationships with other students and staff.

- Create opportunities where all students are developing relationships based on shared positive experiences, such as recreation activities, meals, hobbies, and humor.

- Communicate and document details, so all staff and faculty have timely and accurate information.

- Look for lessons and learn from mistakes.

The Problem: Community Scapegoat

Kim is a thirteen-year-old girl in residential treatment. She struggles with emotional awareness and social skills. Kim is loud, interrupts peers, acts impulsively, has poor self-esteem, misreads social cues, and is hyperfocused in narrow areas of interest (horses and online role-playing games). She engages in repetitive, odd behaviors that are initially humorous but have become tiresome. Despite these difficulties, Kim has genuine goodness about her. She is kind to animals, loves to participate in service projects, and has a fantastic work ethic when she understands what a project entails. Over time, certain members of the community have targeted her with practical jokes and comments that have gone too far.

Kim struggles with being assertive and lacks the skills to effectively set limits with others, resulting in sending mixed messages of how she really feels about the ways others treat her. While Kim receives a significant amount of negative attention, she is grateful to receive any attention from the group. No one wants to be her roommate, and everyone outwardly complains when they are assigned projects with Kim. New students entering the community are told by others to avoid her, and staff passively avoid being directly involved with Kim as well. As a result, group discussions regularly address complaints related to Kim's behaviors.

A new milieu staff member named Renee has just been hired. She is routinely assigned to work with Kim, while other staff members are not. Renee relates to many of Kim's issues and has experienced considerable teasing from others while growing up. Coincidentally, she senses that her coworkers (who have worked with each other for many months or years) are critical of her and are beginning to distance themselves from Renee while on the job.

CONSIDERATIONS FOR SOLUTIONS

The following scene plays out in adolescent lives, whether in treatment settings, private and public schools, or communities across the continuum. Someone with a perceived weakness or difference becomes the odd one out and is inevitably targeted. Instigators are often former recipients of mistreatment themselves but feel they gain power over others through victimization. Participants and bystanders may experience guilt and empathy for victims, yet they passively participate to feel superior and included. They may feel that if they don't participate, they will become the next target.

In public schools, it's difficult to prevent everyday acts of bullying due to a large number of students and limited supervision. Mistreatment is not always observable and often takes place off-campus through cyberbullying, teasing on the bus, etc. A therapeutic environment with fewer residents offers increased structure and supervision, and the majority of student interactions take place on campus. These factors help to reduce the frequency of bullying. As these behaviors occur, treatment settings provide greater immediate focus to actively address problems and to educate in ways that don't typically occur in adolescent life.

When addressing mistreatment among peers, the primary concern is compromised safety in the community. Those who aren't immediate targets may find it difficult to accurately assess the greater implications facing the community. Adolescents struggle to understand how someone else's mistreatment has negative implications for themselves or how these behaviors can become normalized. The majority of residents are not directly impacted, so they may question why they should care or involve themselves in another's problems. The greatest opportunity that exists in these situations is teaching empathy. When students understand they are indirectly affected by another's problems—and they share more similarities with each other than differences—they develop awareness regarding their own behaviors and interactions with others.

Kim would benefit from being assigned solid peer mentors who can provide companionship and supportive feedback on how she is implementing (or not implementing) targeted social skills. Kim possesses certain strengths that contribute positively to the community. These should be harnessed. Sometimes staff and residents develop attentional biases toward problems an individual is experiencing, at the cost of not recognizing what is working well for the individual. Ideally, staff should identify a few of Kim's strengths that her antagonists lack and pair her with those residents, so she can offer support and practice rapport with others.

Another difficulty in this vignette is staff avoiding interactions with Kim after becoming exhausted and annoyed and placing a rookie (Renee) in a primary role with a difficult student. By doing so, staff model the same behaviors that students are engaging in with Kim. Since Renee is a new staff member, she should be involved in regular interactions in which she is learning and observing how senior staff approach and interact with residents. Renee and Kim share similar histories, so their interactions can become triggers—as Renee may reexperience difficult emotions associated with her own negative memories. She may need support to process what is taking place and how her potential emotions can positively or negatively influence her interactions with Kim.

While cliques occur among residents, they also occur among staff. Cliques within the staff lead to certain employees being regularly and passively left out. As a result, those staff members may not receive the emotional support and instruction they need, because differing expectations and double standards create and perpetuate systemic conflicts. Staff conflicts arise from individual and collective problems, just as they do with residents. Imagine a student who has grown up in a dysfunctional household and is now in a program with similar dynamics taking place among staff. These dynamics reflect greater issues that residents and their families experience and may mirror (and trigger) the problems that contributed to therapeutic placement. Therefore, staff and student cliques must be addressed early, as they create divisions that should not be replicated in the program.

Summary

- Teach empathy, respect, compassion, and personal awareness. Model positive ways of gaining attention. Educate students about group identity and norms. Address patterns of creating a community scapegoat. Break the cycle.

- Discuss how hyperfocusing on a community scapegoat enables group members to avoid looking at themselves and addressing their own issues.

- Assign peer mentors to provide support and assist in social learning.

- Initiate team-building activities. Focus on what community members and staff share in common. Recognize that students and staff share similar experiences of being mistreated that can trigger reactivity.

- Review staff and student boundaries regularly.

- Set students up for success. Provide opportunities for the group to benefit from the strengths of individuals.

- Be creative. Model positive attributes that certain students lack. For example, assign students the task of LARPING (live-action role-playing) in which they represent characters with certain abilities or characteristics a student may lack. Process the experience.

- Help students develop increased self-awareness and identify specific social skills that a resident in question can focus on. Offer follow-up feedback (biweekly/monthly) from the community.

- Provide struggling students with increased support and structure during less structured times.

- Demonstrate empathy and emotional intelligence (it's difficult to mistreat others when you see them as vulnerable people). Create opportunities for Kim to share her history with the group, such as where she is from, who is important in her life, etc. Perhaps have Kim's family members write letters to the community expressing how important she is to them or thanking the group for caring about her while she is away (allow Kim to share photos of her family, pets, etc.).

- Initiate opportunities for inexperienced staff to shadow experienced staff before assigning one-on-one roles with students.

- Understand that staff interactions with difficult or challenging students can resemble or mirror similar dynamics occurring in the community.

- Recognize and address staff cliques and conflicts, as they can reflect residents' interactions and community dynamics.

- Be aware that staff conflicts can also resemble issues that have occurred in residents' homes that may become triggers.

- Communicate and document details, so all staff and faculty have timely and accurate information.

- Look for lessons, and learn from mistakes.

The Problem: Anatomically Correct

The following scenario takes place in the community room of a residential treatment center where twelve adolescent males interact with two milieu staff. One staff member is Sara, who has tried to connect with Jack, a struggling student. Earlier in the week, Jack had a blowup with his mother during family therapy and is easily agitated and isolative and has disengaged from the community. For the past three days, Sara has encouraged him to join the others in various activities without success. Jack becomes increasingly annoyed at her efforts to cheer him up. Finally, he agrees to participate in a game with her and four of the other students if they are willing to play a game of his choice afterward.

Sara senses a positive shift as Jack appears more lighthearted, despite the brooding behaviors everyone has observed during the past week. She is encouraged. Before they start the game, residents argue over which game to play. Jack is unhappy with the game the group has chosen and says it is too complicated, has too many rules, is boring, and takes forever to finish. However, the milieu staff and others in the group push back, reminding Jack of their compromise. Sarah states that he needs to honor his commitments in order to improve his relationships with others, particularly with his mother. The feedback doesn't improve his mood. However, Jack reluctantly agrees to play and passively participates in silence for the next 2.5 hours. While the game is coming to a close, the second staff member leaves the room with another student (after he is invited to observe an art project the student is especially proud of). The staff member's exit leaves Sarah with the remaining residents as the first game is completed.

Following a brief break, the students reconvene to play Jack's game. He proposes a version of charades that he played at home with friends. The treatment center does not own the retail version, in which players hold cards with images to their foreheads and group members provide clues to the player's image. Jack suggests they can play without the cards by drawing pictures on each other's foreheads that can be washed off afterward. Participants will earn points as they guess their own pictures. The boys in the group like this idea; however, when Sara questions Jack's proposal, she is met with a chorus of "You made a commitment." Though Jack starts the initial complaints, others join in and add to the onslaught with, "Come on. You made a deal with Jack. Honor your commitments."

Sara is at a crossroads. She doesn't want to appear hypocritical and is concerned about losing Jack's trust and the trust of the group, so she relents. The game proceeds, and Jack and the others are fully engaged. Additional staff members pass through as the game progresses. When it's Sara's turn, Jack takes a marker and draws on her forehead. As he finishes, the boys' expressions range from surprise—to complete shock as the room erupts in sudden, uncontrollable laughter. No one offers Sara any clues about the image drawn on her forehead.

The boys continue to laugh hysterically as she walks to the staff bathroom. Along the way, Sarah is met with more student giggles. A fellow staff member sees her and says, "What happened? Are you OK?" Sara is embarrassed and is afraid to look in the mirror. When she finally glimpses her reflection, she can see that Jack has drawn a penis on her forehead—in marker. Now Sara is mortified. She feels betrayed by Jack and the others. Despite her best efforts to wash the penis drawing from her forehead, the faint image remains, and her face is red from scrubbing. Sarah leaves the bathroom completely humiliated and heads toward the community room to confront Jack.

CONSIDERATIONS FOR SOLUTIONS

Of all the problems described in the chapter, this one appears the most far-fetched. However, the scene is based on actual events. Never underestimate the potential for well-intentioned staff to make miscalculations that lead to a series of unintended outcomes. Over the course of one's lifetime, everyone makes questionable decisions that are clear in hindsight. The scenario presents a number of contributing variables that provide foresight for future planning. The first variable is Sara's genuine care for Jack and sincere desire to help him. While her care is commendable, Sara stepped out of her role as a milieu staff during the unfolding drama. She may have meant well by scolding Jack for his failure to honor commitments; however, the timing was poor, and it isn't Sara's role to comment on Jack's family therapy session. She didn't accurately appraise the situation, and instead of persisting to help Jack, she could have given him space and approached him without a peer audience.

It's possible that if Sara had first established mutual rapport with Jack, he might have heard the message differently or had greater confidence that her intentions were meant to be helpful. Sara's misappraisal and her comment about Jack's family session created potential trust issues between Jack and his primary therapist due to the level of confidentiality that exists in sessions. Though milieu staff members are made privy to certain student issues (in order to prepare for and to anticipate how events may play out in the community), they must remain respectful of confidentiality and their assigned roles.

A critical contributor is the lack of adequate supervision and ratio distribution. Initially, two staff members assisted several students. While this isn't necessarily a ratio violation during a gaming session, numbers suggest that other staff ratios were not properly met across campus. Correct staff-to-student ratios provide appropriate levels of support and reinforce the program's safety and purpose. Ensuring that staff members are correctly positioned and distributed across campus is equally important and should be based on the number of students and the types of activities taking place. For instance, three staff members sitting in a community room while watching a movie with three students is a poor example of spacing and distribution. If there had been better supervision and distribution during the case example, Sara would have had appropriate staff support, and the accompanying scene would have unfolded differently.

The next problem occurs when the other staff member assisting Sara leaves the area to observe a student's artwork. By doing so, he places the needs of the individual student above the safety of the community and his colleagues. Moreover, the assisting staff left a new staff member alone with several students and did not return. If he had remained to play the follow-up game, Jack and other residents would not have teamed up against Sara, and he could have intervened when students began drawing on each other's foreheads. In most situations, it's best to place the needs of the group and community above the requests of an individual. Thus, staff should respond to individual requests when the timing is most advantageous for the community.

Another contributing factor was the length and complexity of the initial game the group chose. Expecting an agitated adolescent to demonstrate the level of frustration tolerance required to complete a 2.5-hour game is unrealistic, and playing an unfamiliar game to appease Jack fueled the fire. After the damage is done, Sara is too upset to have a meaningful and constructive discussion with Jack. At this point, another staff member should intervene, as a confrontation will lead to further issues. While Sara should not have placed herself in a position where a scene like this could occur, Jack is capable of making better decisions and should not be allowed to take advantage of students or staff. He is responsible for his actions, and there must be an appropriate and proportionate response cost. Sara bears the ultimate responsibility for what has occurred. However, the timing of this message to her is important. She needs to be in an emotional headspace where she can accept her mistakes and learn from them. In the immediate moment, Sara needs support from her colleagues and time to process her feelings so she can regroup and finish her shift.

Staff should allow her to take a break or go for a walk. Sara's colleagues should offer encouragement, and she should be contacted later when she is not working to follow up with a supervisor, where she can receive additional support and corrective teaching (documented in her employee file). If she is unable to accept feedback under these circumstances, she may not be suited for a milieu position. The other staff member who left Sara with multiple residents should also be counseled to ensure he understands the importance of staff distribution and student ratios. Consider a formal write-up for this staff member as well, which reinforces safety, employee accountability, and program expectations. Working with adolescent clients is often challenging. However, it's important to remember that residents are in treatment so they can learn and grow. Ultimately, the entire community can benefit positively from negative, isolated incidents and can glean new information that improves ratios, distribution, and best practices.

Summary

- Plan and provide for appropriate supervision and distribution of staff. The most important responsibility of the milieu is to ensure the safety of students. Staff should follow ratio protocols and distribute themselves across campus in accordance with program activities and scheduling.

- Address staff members who seem especially drawn to a student out of a desire to help or who spend disproportionate time and energy assisting a particular student versus others. Provide feedback and corrective teaching from supervisors and colleagues.

- Review and refine job descriptions with staff, so they understand their responsibilities and duties and the parameters associated with their positions. If staff members are taking on responsibilities or roles that are beyond the scope of their positions or training, they should be provided immediate feedback and corrective teaching.

- Teach the importance of appraisal and misappraisal. In the vignette, Sara misunderstands the responsibilities associated with her role, the appropriateness of letting students write on each other (and herself), and the level of rapport she had with Jack. Staff members should be regularly evaluated on their ability to make accurate appraisals (involving self, colleagues, and students) and should be expected to correct errors.

- Address Sara's missed opportunity to teach and model appropriate boundaries when she allowed students to write on each other's foreheads.

- Establish and recommend that certain conversations be held one on one and not in the presence of a peer audience.

- Communicate and document details, so all staff and faculty have timely and accurate information.

- Look for lessons, and learn from mistakes.

Learning from Mistakes

Therapeutic settings offer abundant opportunities for staff to learn and grow while assisting residents to do the same during some of the most difficult times in their lives. The work is challenging but rewarding. Milieu truly matters in any therapeutic setting and is a laboratory for social learning where residents can enhance skill development and formulate healthier habits. While it is important to strive for a professional culture that works proactively to avoid errors, no one appreciates an environment where everyone is in constant fear of making mistakes. Conversely, when isolated incidents are ignored or perpetuated, they become negative patterns that impact the therapeutic process. If harmful patterns are not properly addressed, a program's overall effectiveness decreases, and teaching opportunities are lost.

> Milieu truly matters in any therapeutic setting and is a laboratory for social learning where residents can enhance skill development and formulate healthier habits.

As long as obstacles do not present safety issues, programs can work through and survive isolated incidents that occur along the way. Moreover, problems serve as early warning signs that can lead to positive and lasting changes when properly addressed. Staff must *respond versus react*, and supervisors must provide necessary training and feedback based on the foundational needs of the community. *Everyone* must be willing to learn. Finally, looking for lessons in everyday situations leads to comprehensive refinement that helps programs withstand future problems. Likewise, the entire community benefits from renewed knowledge, skills, and practices. Though success comes in many forms, learning from previous mistakes and diligently striving to improve upon them is at the heart of mental health—and the human experience.

CHAPTER 7

Keeping the Bogeyman Away

Maintaining a Thriving Milieu through Optimal Staff-Management Practices

JARED U. BALMER

S INCE ONE CANNOT *NOT* COMMUNICATE, STAFF AND CLIENTS interact with each other and influence each other continuously in subtle yet profound (and sometimes problematic) ways. This chapter will address the reasons for group collapse as they originate with employee and staff management. Often, a breakdown among employees will lead to a breakdown of the client population and vice versa, leading to a system-wide dysfunction in what can seem like endless perpetuity.

The Problem: Entropy

Creating and maintaining group cohesion, accountability, and support among collections of individuals is not a cakewalk. Individual differences, including personality, temperament, and background, are just a few variables that are at stake when attempting to create group cohesion and unified purpose. Such challenges are particularly in play in the mental health arena, where treatment resistance is an ever-present challenge. Adolescents with behavioral problems are notorious when it comes to projecting their problems outside themselves. They often construe the cause for their maladaptive behavior to be an unreasonable parent or a teacher who "had it in" for them. Because it is not uncommon for such adolescents to push back on taking personal responsibility for what ails them, those in charge of the milieu should take into account that resistant adolescents regularly enter treatment against their better judgment. Mental health professionals have reminded us for decades that virtually all individuals resist change for one reason or another. Thus, overcoming resistance is at the core of a purposeful group process that aims for behavioral change.

For decades social psychologists have explored the processes that lead social groups of all kinds to achieve oneness and uniformity. Questions like "How do groups transmit and share norms and standards?" have been investigated. Others have studied how group members obey authorities and respond to the pressure to conform.

> Regardless of the psychosocial history, levels of acuity, diagnosis, or presenting problems, all groups demonstrate fluctuating levels of resistance. If left alone without vigilant attention from the professional staff, all groups tend to break down.

The conclusion of these and related studies shows that despite a tendency to cohere and to seek consensus, virtually all social groups are internally divided into subgroups. And what is even more significant is that these studies indicate that often members of a subgroup may decide to leave the parent group, either to form a breakaway group or to join a different group. Such breakdowns of group cohesion are principally fueled by resistance.

Regardless of the psychosocial history, levels of acuity, diagnosis, or presenting problems, all groups demonstrate fluctuating levels of resistance. If left alone without vigilant attention from the professional staff, all groups tend to break down. In that regard, groups are subject to the second law of thermodynamics, which states there is a natural tendency of any isolated system to degenerate into a more disordered state. In the social realms of which we speak, entropy, the natural tendency of group or milieu breakdown, is a force that demands constant attention.

Preventing Milieu Breakdowns from the Staff Perspective

Preventing therapeutic group breakdowns demands hypervigilant attention from the caregivers. In a day-treatment setting, observation begins upon arrival and ends at the departure of the group members. In a residential setting, paying attention to client interactions takes place around the clock. Indeed, disturbances in the milieu can flourish under the cloak of darkness. There is no end to all the potential reasons for, and times of, a dysfunctional milieu. Anticipating such interfering forces through proactive measures will keep the milieu therapeutically healthy, which is the aim of establishing a supportive environment where group members are accountable to themselves and others. Below are critical considerations for the prevention of milieu breakdowns and possible solutions for optimal functioning.

WHOM DO WE SERVE?

Mental health programs in all their varieties are best administered by having a clear understating of whom they intend to serve. As mentioned in a previous chapter, such understanding cannot be restricted to the memories of a few key stakeholders but must be clearly written in a policy and available to all staff. Long before opening the door to new admissions, program operators must devote attention to the *core* aspects of the program, which include such topics as the following:

- A mission statement

- The service philosophy

- The goals and objectives of the program

- The theoretical foundation of the treatment

- A description of the population served

- Exclusion and discharge criteria

- Rational delineation of core therapeutic services upon which the change process is pivoting

Equally important is a clear description of the rules, guidelines, and expectations of the therapeutic milieu—the daily traffic rules of the coming and going of the clients.

TRAINING, TRAINING, TRAINING

Ensuring that all staff members are intricately familiar with the milieu policy, guidelines, and rules is the first defense against group entropy. During the genesis of a newly formed treatment milieu, staff training is typically a well-established practice. However, during the ensuing months and years, that which was clear may begin to fade and become murky. The answer is training. However, training has its own challenges. Depending on the number of staff within a given operation, intervals of training sessions can have a great range in frequency. This might be a familiar question to those who run a facility: "Do we train a single new employee now, or do we wait until we have a greater number to train?" Could this potential delay go on for weeks, where the budding employee is theoretically groping in the dark? In another scenario, typically, the nonprofessional staff are assigned to monitor the milieu. In the majority of cases, these staff members have the least formal education and will therefore benefit the most from ongoing training. In a simplified but effective way to train, as new employees report to work, and as more seasoned employees show the need for a tune-up, videos can be a useful way to keep employees current with orientation and training requirements. Such videos are easily produced by key leadership, uploaded on a computer platform, and viewed. Along with the video, a written test may provide assurance that the topic is understood, therefore establishing a measure of competency associated with the training topic.

STACKING THE DECK

It is no great secret that a single bad apple in a bushel of apples has a way of infecting the others. Carefully vetting the history of new group members pays great dividends. Such vetting is done by reviewing the fit of the new client against the admission and exclusion criteria. While this must be crucial standard practice, at times, an unfortunate issue may arise. It is possible for a client's history to be inaccurate, with critical information missing or added. This makes it difficult for admission decision makers to find the proper fit. In that regard, the information source must be considered and examined for possible biases, lack of insight, or lack of knowledge about important historical data. Important as it is, such a vetting process is no guarantee that a new group member will not have a negative effect on the milieu. After weeks or months following admission, behavior may creep up in a client that will test the integrity of the milieu. A thorough vetting process, holding tightly to the admission and exclusion criteria, is stacking the deck in the right direction. Financial stakeholders must not fall prey to the demands of profitability by turning a blind eye to the vetting process, especially for programs trying to establish a solid reputation for integrity. When weighed in the balance, milieu breakdown via poor vetting is a senseless cost. Once fully established, with optimal milieu functioning, a program may venture beyond the narrow admission criteria. Such decisions are made by a close examination of the strength of the positive leadership among the client population.

FINDING HOLES

Milieu rules and guidelines have ways of changing over time. This is particularly the case in the early months and years of a newly established program. Such adjustments are inevitably the results of certain clients who cleverly find holes to thread behaviors that are beneficial neither for them individually nor for the group. Unattended, such deviations from the rule book are often the genesis for group entropy. It is precisely such behaviors that provide the stakeholders an opportunity to fine-tune the milieu rules and guidelines—a welcome activity. Take care, however. Weekly or daily adjustments and changes to the milieu rules can be detrimental. The confusion invites deviant behavior and encourages group breakdowns. Moreover, it signals that the authors of the milieu program did not sufficiently consider the types of clients they intended to serve. In that regard, it is always easier to start with more stringent rules and guidelines. A client's response to lowering the bar is seen as favorable and viewed as a reward. To rectify loose rules by adding pages to the rulebook is viewed as punishment. Missing the mark on establishing the rules and guidelines of the milieu has long-term consequences that can never be completely rectified.

TRENCH WARFARE

Military experts tell us the soldier on the ground is always right. This truism implies that officers and general corps may, at times, be at odds with the soldiers in the trenches. For a mental health operation to be successful, there can be no rift between the leadership and those who spend the most time with the clients. Such a schism is easily detected by the patients and fuels group breakdowns. For an organization to be successful, each member needs to know their contribution matters. The frontline worker, who is the soldier in the trenches, will not realize this intuitively. He or she needs more kudos than a sign that hangs in the lobby. The employees who are responsible for the direct supervision and guidance of the milieu need to feel welcomed and appreciated. This is facilitated through the practice of a working environment where communication is open and honest—a climate in which team members are appreciated for a wise critique and never punished for speaking up about a perceived problem. Periodic one-on-one meetings with the leadership team can engender invaluable benefits, sending the message of a united front to program participants.

> For an organization to be successful, each member needs to know their contribution matters.

CLARITY IS A WINNER

Clients have a knack for reading the program culture like a book. They are attuned to observing verbal and nonverbal cues from their caretakers. Until such clients are established in a routine of improvement, any discrepancy among the caretakers charged with supervising the milieu is exploited to a potential deviant advantage. This can lead to "staff shopping," the practice of finding staff members who will provide the most favorable answers or interpretation of milieu rules and guidelines. When different staff members react with variability to clients' issues and requests, confusion and the breakdown of the group cohesion follow suit. At its core, the antidote for such a breakdown is to have clarity of job roles and responsibilities. Assuring that all staff members are "singing from the same page" *all the time* starts with a detailed job description. In that regard, researchers have found that small companies fall into the trap of lacking specificity in delineating roles and responsibilities. They dislike spending time immersed in paperwork. Unfortunately, there may be an attitude that, for them, such bureaucracy is not necessary since "we can simply talk to each other." While we agree that talk is good, talking without a written job description negatively facilitates a by-the-seat-of-your-pants method of responsibilities delineation. In addition, small companies have employees who must take on more than one role, which in turn complicates the written production of an understandable job description. While it may be attractive for employees to wear multiple hats, it can be a major cause of team breakdown. Why? Who wears the hat on what day? From day to day, does passing the hat cause a confusing range of responsibilities? In bigger companies, some employees could rise up and say, "This is not my job," failing to snap to attention when some action is needed. With endless emerging issues within the milieu, there is a requisite demand for fluidity. Along with clear-cut job descriptions, companies large and small must consider the importance of cross-training. What builds stamina at the gym applies to the strength of the milieu.

MILIEU STAFF LEADERSHIP

Lack of leadership is one of the primary reasons for group breakdowns. Every group of individuals pursuing personal growth needs a leader who sets expectations and keeps clients and staff focused on the collective group goals. More often, such leaders are not made; they are born. Despite poring over endless books on management and participating in formal training, leadership is very often an innate talent. Stakeholders should look for this quality and recognize it as they staff the milieu. An effective leader employs positive reinforcement to keep the workforce motivated. He or she is taking the temperature of the employees' morale and engages in various cheerleading activities. This is best done on an intermittent basis and not only when the chips are down. A team leader also needs to hold people accountable. This does not equate to a leadership style that is tough, harsh, or unbending—a style indicative of someone who is unsure of his or her leadership capabilities. Accountability means setting clear benchmarks and expectations, being fair, not showing favoritism, and expecting excellent work. It's good to remember that team leaders set the standard and live by it. You may have a staff member who does not pull his or her own weight, is chronically tardy, or demonstrates performance problems. Don't ignore the problem. Address it quickly, and then move to secure a friendly demeanor by pointing out the employee's admirable qualities. (Hopefully, the person has some.) Being a cheerleader, one who uses enthusiasm on the one hand and demands accountability on the other, is not showing signs of schizophrenia. A great leader is defined by the optimal application of both—cheerleading and the expectation of accountability. Such a leadership style demands respect. When warning signs appear of team breakdowns, smart leaders will engage in root-cause analysis. Every stone is turned over to look for clues of what might be amiss, including their own involvement.

FAVORITISM, NEPOTISM, AND CRONYISM

Some of us can remember teachers in an educational setting who had one or two pet students to whom they showed favoritism over the rest of the class. Others may remember losing a job promotion to the boss's nephew. In both cases, the net result was that we hated both the teacher, the boss, and the favored pet(s). The same result is present among members of a working team on which the team leader plays favorites. Favoritism manifests in different ways. Allowing certain individuals to report late or leave early from work or permitting a favorite employee not to "get their hands dirty" are all obviously inappropriate but happen nonetheless. How would it play for the rest of the team when the group leader invites one employee—time and time again—on a fly-fishing excursion? Better yet, upon returning, what if they share photos of the trip with the rest of the team? Sharing outside interests among team members may very well add to team spirit. However, such activities between supervisors and subordinates can take on a different meaning. Something as simple as a regular smoke break with a certain team member can appear dicey to others, giving rise to suspicion and resentment. In the minds of fellow team members, such a subordinate may rise to the level of "untouchable," having forged a special relationship with the boss. The spotlight on special relationships becomes more problematic when the supervisor and the employee are family members. Even when great care is taken to prevent favoritism, the obvious singularity of family relationships within the same department is tricky and should be avoided. The generosity of a Christmas turkey cannot make amends for the carelessness of partiality. It goes without saying that the negative effect on the team is the same when leaders themselves engage in privileged behaviors.

COMPETITION AS A MOTIVATOR

There is no shortage of books that espouse the value of employing competition as a motivator. We see it especially across the athletic landscape. There are various country Olympic teams, the varsity and the practice teams, the major and minor leagues, the starters and the benchwarmers. Such efforts to increase performance may be well suited to reach a particular *individual* goal. However, during team meetings in the workplace, celebrating the achievement of a single person in the hopes of motivating others may result in resentment of the team leader and possible jealousy of the "winner." Singing the praise of the same individual repeatedly is a formula for team breakdowns. Building a strong team is predicated on the notion that all team members feel they contribute and are recognized for the overall goals of the team. Acknowledging the individual achievements of team members can contribute to a strong team identity if all team members are inducted into the hall of fame. The kryptonite for team spirit and culture is in full force when group members are under the impression there exists a ranking from the best to the worst team member. Group cohesion is achieved when members want to make their peers look good—an accomplishment that defines a healthy team.

FEAR OF FAILURE

Fear can be a valuable motivator. Fear of failure may propel a student into an additional hour of study in the hopes of improving the grade on the final exam. However, when fear exceeds the capacity to respond appropriately, failure will ensue in short order. Most employee handbooks delineate unacceptable behaviors that may lead to dismissal—perhaps evoking a fear response. Supervisors need to live by the rule book and also create a working climate that encourages innovation, new ways to solve problems, and creativity. It is not uncommon for some employees to feel anxiety over bringing up an idea that ventures into uncharted territory. The thought that one may look stupid or incompetent can stymie any opinions of new and improved ways for problem solving. It is also fairly common for new employees *not* to ask questions of their respective supervisors on account that asking questions may be a sign of ignorance, casting the employee in a less-than-favorable light. The antidote for this misguided perception is the supervisor's message that asking questions is a sign of "I want to learn" and is empowering.

THE ENDLESS DEMAND FOR COMMUNICATION

Employee feedback questionnaires have been circulated for centuries throughout organizations and businesses in all their varieties. The standard question is always the same: "What suggestions do you have for improvements?" The overwhelming response to this question is "Improve communication." The demand to be in the know increases with the size, complexity, and number of employees within the organization. What is particularly challenging is when the organization is operating with multiple shifts. Ensuring that accurate and complete information is passed along between a day, afternoon, and night shift can be solved by either a short shift overlay or written/electronic communication logs that are required reading. Such an exchange of data does not diminish the need for regular and formal team meetings in which employees can exchange information and problem solve in an open and honest setting.

THE DISRUPTER

An unhappy or disgruntled employee can cause a mountain of problems. This is particularly the case if such an individual is directly working with the client population. There is no end to the different possibilities of what ails an employee. It can range from compensation issues to a personal injury that occurred on the job and everything imaginable in between. In most cases, such unhappiness is manifested in conduct and job performance. Unchecked, a single individual can cause damage to both the staff team and the therapeutic milieu. It may take months or years to rectify. In the behavioral science arena, supervisors and stakeholders often go the extra mile to reform the disrupter, only to find it is futile. If the reformation process does not bear fruit in a short timeframe, ending the employment for the disrupter is the only option to preserve the team spirit among employees and the client population.

GROWING STALE

Growing stale as a company has two origins. The first problem is employees who feel overwhelmed and are trying their best to avoid burnout. It is not stress that is the cause of burnout; it is *distress*. What is the difference between stress and distress? An optimal amount of stress can increase work performance. We visit the gym and put our bodies under stress in hopes of increasing physical performance. We are in distress when the fifty-pound dumbbell drops on our toe. A workforce in distress deals with survival, hanging on to the job, and shirking assignments and follow-through. Distress leads to entropy. The phenomenon of burnout has long been addressed in professional literature and is particularly relevant in the helping professions. An impressive number of employees who work with those experiencing emotional and mental pain find themselves reacting with distress. Compassion fatigue is real and should never be overlooked by employers concerned with the bottom line. Caregivers who are running out of oxygen are as much a bottom-line issue as rent and other financial obligations. Prevention would include intentional actions via training, self-advocacy, or some time off. Another measure would be through a peer support system. When peers notice impairment or changes in behavior, they can step in and help with "life support."

Second, reinventing oneself is not an extravagance in behavioral health; it is the crucial antidote for growing stale. The state of the art in behavioral health is largely determined by an ever-growing and expanding supply of research. The landscape of best practices is continually evolving, resulting in new and improved ways of patient care. Organizations that are under the illusion they possess the holy grail in treating a particular disorder may soon find their freshness has expired. Associations that operate under the philosophy of constant improvement—and incentivize employees to look for such improvements—find an energized workforce ready to embrace positive change.

BONDING THROUGH CHALLENGES

In every town and city, small or large, there is a VFW building. VFW stands for Veterans of Foreign Wars, and the building is a place where soldiers meet and socialize. The bonds among those who experienced challenges together is a powerful force. Not unlike veterans, employees of organizations that face challenges have a great opportunity for bonding—coming together, unified in purpose to achieve a common goal. That common goal often can be strained by organizational, departmental, or service area challenges. A pandemic, a suicide attempt, runaways, a disruption of the water supply, and the need to break up a toxic group of clients are just a small sampling. Challenges are opportunities for each employee to take on the responsibilities of a stakeholder, invest in empowerment, and contribute to the welfare of the organization.

Summary

Entropy, a law of nature, is a tendency of any group to break down. Entropy is as real as gravity. The difference between entropy and gravity is that hypervigilant attention to the milieu can keep the forces of entropy at bay.

Throughout this book, multiple challenges have been discussed. There are a hundred more. The problems we highlighted here we have experienced ourselves or observed in other settings. Some were easily solved. Others caused heartache and, during some extraordinary circumstances, a few sleepless nights. Encountering problems and setbacks and solving them made us stronger and, hopefully, wiser. A new baby born to a family does not come with a manual of instruction. In the late seventies and early eighties, when we birthed our first treatment environments—which combined education, psychotherapy, recreation, and psychiatry under one roof—we wish a book like this had been available to us. We think you'll find it helpful and truly wish you a productive reading experience. May the force be with you.

CPSIA information can be obtained
at www.ICGtesting.com
Printed in the USA
FSHW022309051221

9 781642 253436